Things that Jesus did
Miracles of the Kingdom & Signs of Eternal Life

Doug Rowston

Rowston, Doug
THINGS THAT JESUS DID
Miracles of the Kingdom & Signs of Eternal Life

Published by
Grace & Peace Books
4A Wurilba Ave Hawthorn SA 5062 Australia
djrowston@gmail.com

© Douglas James Rowston 2018

This work is copyright. Other than for the purposes and subject to the conditions prescribed under the Copyright Act, no part of it may in any form or by any means (electronic, mechanical, microcopying, photocopying, recording or otherwise) be reproduced, stored in a retrieval system or transmitted without prior written permission from the publisher.

First published 2018 by MediaCom Education Inc
This edition published in 2022

ISBN 978-0-6453288-6-8

This book is dedicated to

Norm Bennett

with whom it was my privilege

to teach religious education

for sixteen years

A significant proportion of the Gospels narrate the actions of Jesus. What Jesus did is integral to his mission and ministry, and Doug Rowston's most helpful overview guides the reader into perceiving deeper meanings and truths that form our gospel traditions. Providing just enough background information, Rowston adeptly places the passages in context, while ensuring the power of these narratives stays much in the foreground. Accessible for those seeking an introduction, and with some great insights for those more familiar with such passages, this new book continues like the earlier *Things that Jesus said* to take the reader on a pilgrimage of sorts, drawn further along following the footsteps of Jesus on a journey still underway.

Bishop Tim Harris
Research Fellow St Barnabas College

Doug Rowston's *Things that Jesus did* brings his considerable scholarship alongside personal stories and reflections from believers throughout the centuries to invite readers to both understand and experience the miracle stories of the gospels. He draws on insights from archaeology, geography, and history to provide helpful background commentary, but his real strength in his ability to weave personal stories – of his own, those he has met, and those both known and obscure to history – to offer an invitation to the reader to engage their imagination, enter into the events, and therein encounter Jesus. His simple reflections and humble prayers at the conclusion of each story serve as a profound reminder that these stories can be encountered again and again.

Rev Dr Melinda Cousins
Director of Ministries Baptist Churches of SA

Acknowledgements

The front cover is a mosaic of Christ and the Gospel at the Monastery of Hosios Lucas on the slopes of Mount Helikon in Greece.

The ink sketches throughout the book were drawn by Craig Bowyer during the author's time as teacher at Prince Alfred College in Adelaide. They are reproduced with his permission.

Bible quotations are from the New Revised Standard Version Bible, copyright 1989, 1995 by the Division of Christian Education of the National Council of Churches of Christ in the U S A. Used by permission. All rights reserved.

Contents

Introduction		1
Part 1: Miracles in Matthew's Gospel		5
1	A Leper	6
2	A Centurion's Servant	11
3	Peter's Mother-in-law	17
4	A Gale	23
5	A Paralysed Man	28
6	A Woman and a Girl	32
Part 2: Miracles in Mark's Gospel		37
7	A Gerasene Demoniac	38
8	A Syrophoenician Woman	44
9	A Deaf and Dumb Man	49
10	A Blind Man	54
11	An Epileptic Boy	59
12	Blind Bartimaeus	66
Part 3: Miracles in Luke's Gospel		71
13	A Catch of Fish	72
14	A Widow's Son	82
15	A Crippled Woman	88
16	A Swollen Man	94
17	Ten Lepers	98
18	A Stranger on the Road	106

Part 4: Signs in John's Gospel   **114**

19	A Wedding	115
20	A Royal Official	121
21	A Lame Man	125
22	A Large Crowd	132
23	The Lake	139
24	A Blind Man	144
25	Dead Lazarus	149
26	Doubting Thomas	156
27	A Stranger on the Shore	163

Conclusion   **170**

Select Bibliography   **173**

Introduction

Things that Jesus did is an attempt to take seriously the stories about Jesus in the Four Gospels. Not only is Jesus remembered for the stories he told, but he is also famous for stories about his healing of people who suffered from leprosy, paralysis, fever, haemorrhages, physical handicaps, demonic possession, epilepsy, deafness and dumbness, blindness, and lameness. Furthermore, he is the central character in stories told about nature miracles such as stilling storms, multiplying loaves and fishes, even abnormal catches of fish, and even water turning into wine. Most amazingly, Jesus is credited with raising dead people, let alone being raised from the dead himself.

What are we in the twenty-first century to make of these stories about Jesus which took place in the first century? We belong to an era with a modern scientific worldview. Today there are non-believing scientists and historians who think that they can explain everything without recourse to God. But this is not the whole story. There are believing scientists who see both the mysterious work of God through the microscope and the majestic work of God through the telescope. Similarly, there are believing historians who acknowledge the importance of both the memorable words of Jesus and his mighty works in the Gospels.

All of this is a far cry from the first century context of a pre-scientific worldview. The ancients tended to attribute events and processes to the direct influence of good or evil powers. They felt themselves at the mercy of fate and death. They engaged in superstitious rituals to manipulate the unseen spirits and demons. Despite sharing a pre-scientific worldview, the followers of Jesus rejected an unresolved dualism of good and evil. Good and evil forces were in conflict as Jesus challenged his world. But Jesus was the ultimate victor over evil and death. His followers came to acknowledge the coming of God's rule in the works and words of Jesus and to await Jesus' final glorious reign.

While we do not share the pre-scientific worldview, we can still empathise with the ways in which the Gospels tell the stories of Jesus' miracles and signs. While we seek many answers about what happened from a scientific worldview, we shall find it more helpful to move to the issue of the actual meaning of the miracles for ancient and modern readers of the Gospels.

According to Alan Culpepper, the miracle stories may serve five functions in the Gospels.[1] First, in terms of God, 'the miracle stories ... are signs of God's power and glory.' Second, in relation to Christ, 'the miracles tell us who Jesus was.' Third, in the interpretation of the Bible, 'the miracle stories ... link Jesus to "the Law and the prophets" and show that he was the fulfilment of the Hebrew Scriptures.' Fourth, as part of the church's proclamation, 'the miracle stories often ... demonstrate the power of Jesus' word.' Fifth, as part of the church's instruction, 'the miracle stories often ... offer a lesson on discipleship.'

The miracles told in the First Three Gospels are indications of the coming of the reign of God in the life of Jesus. When his predecessor asked if Jesus was the one for whom they were waiting, Jesus sent John the Baptist this message, *'Go and tell*

---

[1] R. Alan Culpepper, *Mark*, pp. 68-70.

John what you hear and see: the blind receive their sight, the lame walk, the lepers are cleansed, the deaf hear, the dead are raised, and the poor have good news brought to them. And blessed is anyone who takes no offence at me.' (Matthew 11:4-5)

The signs recorded in the Fourth Gospel are revelations of the splendour of God in his Son, the Messiah. When the editor of the Fourth Gospel summed up his testimony, he wrote: *Jesus did many other signs in the presence of his disciples, which are not written in this book. But these are written so that you may come to believe that Jesus is the Messiah, the Son of God, and that through believing you may have life in his name. (John 20:30-31)*

What are we to make of this variety of miracles or signs? Are they for us interventions by the outside Creator into his creation? Are they powerful acts of the unseen yet present Creator within his creation? In his insightful *For Everyone* series Tom Wright seems to bridge the pre-scientific and scientific worldview when he writes,

Our word 'miracle' tends to imply that God, normally 'outside' the closed system of the world, sometimes 'intervenes'; miracles have then frequently been denied by sceptics as a matter of principle. However, in the Bible God is always present, however strangely, and 'deeds of power' are seen as *special* acts of a *present* God rather than *intrusive* acts of an *absent* one.[2]

I trust that this book will encourage you my readers to take seriously the variety of stories about Jesus found in the Four

---

[2] Tom Wright, *Matthew for Everyone*, 1:215-216. This comment appears in the glossary at the end of each volume in this excellent series on the New Testament.

Gospels. It is worth reminding ourselves that the first followers of Jesus learned to appreciate him as God who is there. May we see him as the God who is with us, indeed God's very Son. Not only can we read and appreciate his unforgettable words but we too can treasure the records of his life-changing deeds. In him God's heaven and humankind's earth are joined; in him God's future continues to transform humankind's present. No wonder that for two thousand years known and unknown followers of Jesus, including theologians, evangelists, preachers, writers, poets, rebels, missionaries, mystics, activists, scholars, and martyrs have each in their own way testified in word and deed to this Jesus, the Word made flesh.

Like my previous book, *Things that Jesus said,* the present book comes from my experience as a theological lecturer at Burleigh College, a religious education teacher at Prince Alfred College, a pastor at Richmond Baptist Church, and an adjunct lecturer at St Barnabas College (Charles Sturt University). I have also been helped by the usual suspects in the world of academia as the bibliography will reveal. I thank my wife Rosalie for her companionship and support. I am also grateful to my brother Laurie for his reading and critique of this project as a work in progress. I trust that *Things that Jesus did* will be interesting and enjoyable reading for seekers either as individuals or groups enquiring further after the truth as it is in Jesus.

Doug Rowston

Part 1: Miracles in Matthew's Gospel

A Prayer for Readers of Matthew's Gospel[1]

Living God of Matthew's Good News about Jesus, we thank you for Jesus, the human face of God and the great teacher. Make us sensitive to this human face and enable us to be obedient to his insightful teaching. We are grateful that Jesus was God with us and that he is still with us, to the very end. Amen.

---

[1] Doug Rowston, *A Bird's Eye View of the Bible Second Edition*, p. 139.

1   A Leper

When Jesus had come down from the mountain, great crowds followed him; and there was a leper who came to him and knelt before him, saying, 'Lord, if you choose, you can make me clean.' He stretched out his hand and touched him, saying, 'I do choose. Be made clean!' Immediately his leprosy was cleansed. Then Jesus said to him, 'See that you say nothing to anyone; but go, show yourself to the priest, and offer the gift that Moses commanded, as a testimony to them.'
(Matthew 8:1-4; compare Mark 1:40-45; Luke 5:12-16; Aland, *Synopsis* ## 42, 84)

Telling the Story

Jesus had come down from the mountain. Matthew tells the story after his collection of the teaching of Jesus which we call the Sermon on the Mount. Jesus who has been portrayed as Messiah in word is now shown to be Messiah in deed. In front of great crowds *a leper* comes to Jesus, falls down, and pleads for help. The word *leprosy* in the Bible 'may at times refer to what is generally termed leprosy, but probability extends to such skin diseases as psoriasis, lupus, ringworm, and favus, and in the absence of more precise data it is best to use the more general term **serious skin disease**.'[1] As Leviticus 13:45-46 says, *The person who has the leprous disease shall wear torn clothes and let the hair of his head be dishevelled; and he shall cover his upper lip and cry out, 'Unclean, unclean.' He shall remain unclean as long as he has the disease; he is unclean. He shall live alone; his dwelling shall be outside the camp.*

---

[1] Bauer et al., *A Greek-English Lexicon of the New Testament*, p. 592.

Yet this poor isolated man with the serious skin disease says, *'Lord, if you choose, you can make me clean.'* He trusts Jesus as Lord, the one who can rid him of the disease. Jesus is willing to oblige by touching the untouchable man. *He stretched out his hand and touched him.* He is also willing to oblige by saying the cleansing word. *'I do choose. Be made clean!'* Then he commands the healed man to say nothing to anyone but to go and show himself to the priest and offer a gift of thanks. According to Leviticus 14:4-7, *The priest shall command that two living clean birds ... be brought for the one who is to be cleansed. The priest shall command that one of the birds be slaughtered over fresh water in an earthen vessel. He shall take the living bird ... and dip the living bird in the blood of the bird that was slaughtered over the fresh water. He shall sprinkle it seven times upon the one who is to be cleansed ... then he shall pronounce him clean, and he shall let the living bird go into the open field.*

At the command of Jesus the healed man does all this *as a testimony to them.* That is to say, it is a witness to the people or the priests. The readers of Matthew are reminded that Jesus is fulfilling the purpose of the law and the prophets as he says, *Do not think that I have come to abolish the law or the prophets; I have come not to abolish but to fulfil. (Matthew 5:17)* Matthew also reminds his readers of the words and deeds of Jesus the Messiah in the message given to the imprisoned John the Baptist, *'Go and tell John what you hear and see: the blind receive their sight, the lame walk, the lepers are cleansed, the deaf hear, the dead are raised, and the poor have good news brought to them. And blessed is anyone who takes no offence at me.'(Matthew 11:4-6)*

Interpreting the Story

Matthew has edited and abbreviated Mark's account. Mark included the story after a day of healings in Capernaum. According to Mark, somewhere in Galilee Jesus encounters the leper. Unlike Matthew and Luke, Mark notes that Jesus was *moved with pity*[2] as he *stretched out his hand and touched him, and said to him, 'I do choose. Be made clean!'* Like Matthew and Luke, Mark notes that the leper was healed *immediately*. However, according to Mark, contrary to the instruction of Jesus, *he went out and began to proclaim it freely, and to spread the word, so that Jesus ... stayed out in the country; and people came to him from every quarter.*

Luke has refined Mark's account, including the story in a Galilean tour of Jesus *in one of the cities*. Like Matthew but unlike Mark, Luke does two things. He uses the word traditionally translated *Behold!* and notes that the leper addresses Jesus as *Lord*. At the end of the story Luke broadens the effect of the healing: *But now more than ever the word about Jesus spread abroad; many crowds would gather to hear him and to be cured of their diseases.* Luke also mentions the desire of Jesus for solitude: *But he would withdraw to deserted places and pray.*

---

[2] A variant reading is in a minority of manuscripts: *moved with anger*. Possibly this represents an understanding that Jesus was angry with the disease. The majority reading - *moved with pity* - is accepted by most modern translations.

Experiencing the Story

Historically, the healing ministry of Jesus of so-called lepers has influenced both Roman Catholics and Protestants. In the second half of the nineteenth century the Belgian Catholic priest Father Damien on Molokai Island in Hawaii and the Irish Protestant teacher Wellesley Bailey in the Punjab in India began work among lepers.

Between 1864 and 1889 Father Damien improved the living conditions of the sufferers of the dread disease, indeed shared their existence before he died of leprosy at the age of 49. Subsequently Father Damien was recognised by the Roman Church as a saint and is called the Apostle of the Lepers. Father Damien reflected on his plight as a fellow leper: 'Although there are scientists searching for the cause of this deadly disease and perhaps they will, one day, discover a treatment, at the moment, there is nothing. It is a death sentence. That is why they, we, are here on Molokai. My beloved lepers were sent here, away from their families and friends, abandoning their homes and all that they loved, so that they could be isolated'.[3]

Wellesley Bailey too, with the support of Irish Christians, discovered the plight of lepers and founded a mission to care for lepers. In his own words, 'I almost shuddered... yet at the same time [I was] fascinated, and I felt, if ever there was a Christ–like work in the world it was to go amongst these poor sufferers and bring them the consolation, the hope of the gospel'.[4] Between 1874 and 1893 Wellesley and Alice Bailey

---

[3] www.catholicmission.org.au

[4] www.leprosymission.org.uk

worked throughout India among lepers. In the 1940s and 1950s the Leprosy Mission's effectiveness was enhanced by Paul Brand's medical research in South India. Since then the Leprosy Mission has been at the forefront of the development of new drugs to cure the disease.

Pastorally, the care of Jesus for the suffering outcasts in ancient times has motivated his followers down through the years of Christian history to care for the poor, the needy, the sick and the dying. Like Jesus, his followers have looked upon such people and *had compassion for them, because they were harassed and helpless, like sheep without a shepherd. (Matthew 9:36)*

Reflection

Think about notable figures of faith in medical work such as the Leprosy Mission.

Prayer

Lord, here are our lives which we place on the altar of sacrificial service for you to use as you will in the spirit of the compassionate Christ. Amen.

2 A Centurion's Servant

When he entered Capernaum, a centurion came to him, appealing to him and saying, 'Lord, my servant is lying at home paralysed, in terrible distress.' And he said to him, 'I will come and cure him.' The centurion answered, 'Lord, I am not worthy to have you come under my roof; but only speak the word, and my servant will be healed. For I also am a man under authority, with soldiers under me; and I say to one, 'Go,' and he goes, and to another, 'Come,' and he comes, and to my slave, 'Do this,' and the slave does it.' When Jesus heard him, he was amazed and said to those who followed him, 'Truly I tell you, in no one in Israel have I found such faith. I tell you, many will come from east and west and will eat with Abraham and Isaac and Jacob in the kingdom of heaven, while the heirs of the kingdom will be thrown into the outer darkness, where there will be weeping and gnashing of teeth.' And to the centurion Jesus said, 'Go; let it be done for you according to your faith.' And the servant was healed in that hour.
(Matthew 8:5-13; compare Luke 7:1-10; Aland, *Synopsis* # 85)

Telling the Story

Matthew continues his collection of miracle stories by telling about an encounter with a Roman centurion at Capernaum. It is a story which Matthew and Luke both share in their Gospels, with Matthew's version shorter than Luke's. According to Matthew, Jesus enters into Capernaum and is met by an anxious army officer. A dialogue ensues. The centurion says, '*Lord, my servant* [Greek, *pais*] *is lying at home paralysed, in terrible distress.*' Jesus responds, '*I will come and cure him.*' The centurion shows deep humility and amazing trust, '*Lord, I am not worthy to have you come under my roof; but only speak the word, and my servant will be healed.*' Furthermore, the centurion admits that he understands his own earthly authority and implies faith in the heavenly authority of Jesus. Jesus then speaks to the onlookers, '*Truly I tell you, in no one in Israel have I found such faith.*' Moreover, Jesus contrasts the faith of this Gentile, one of many who *will come from east and west,* with the lack of faith on the part of *the heirs of the kingdom*, who fail to welcome Jesus the Messiah. Jesus once again turns his attention to the centurion and his servant, *'Go; let it be done for you according to your faith.'* Accordingly, the servant recovers his health at that time.

'Lord, I am not worthy to have you come under my roof; but only speak the word, and my servant will be healed.'

Interpreting the Story

Both Matthew and Luke set the incident on the north-west shore of Lake Galilee in Capernaum, in Hebrew 'Kephar

Nahum', meaning 'Village of Nahum'[1]. As we shall see in the next story about Peter's mother-in-law, Capernaum is known today as the site of Peter's house. Capernaum also features the ruins of a synagogue, which date from the 4th-5th century and may have been built over a 1st century structure. Both evangelists highlight the role of a centurion. Such a man had control over a hundred soldiers. It is likely that he was a Gentile officer in the army of Herod Antipas, the ruler of Galilee and Perea. As such it is unlikely that he shared the experiences of a Jew. He had not been circumcised, he had not kept Jewish food laws, he had not grown up observing the sabbath, and he had not participated in the sacrificial practices of the Jerusalem Temple. However, he had learned to respect the history and culture of the Jews in Capernaum so much so that he paid for the building of their synagogue. He was probably a 'God fearer' who accepted the moral teaching of the Jewish Scriptures.

In Luke the centurion is portrayed as sending elders from the Jewish synagogue to intercede on behalf of his servant. Although the centurion is a Gentile, he is drawn to the Jewish faith. The elders ask Jesus to come and heal his *slave* [Greek, *doulos*]. He is obviously a benevolent master as well as a generous Gentile. As the elders say, *'He is worthy of having you do this for him, for he loves our people, and it is he who built our synagogue for us.'* When Jesus comes near the centurion's house, the centurion sends friends with a message, *'Lord, do not trouble yourself, for I am not worthy to have you come under my roof; therefore I did not presume to come to*

---

[1] John C.H. Laughlin, 'Capernaum', *The New Interpreter's Dictionary of the Bible*, 1:564-566.

you. But only speak the word, and let my servant be healed.' According to Luke, Jesus praises the centurion in similar terms to Matthew: *'I tell you, not even in Israel have I found such faith.'* Luke concludes with the statement: *When those who had been sent returned to the house, they found the slave in good health.*

Experiencing the Story

Whether the centurion encounters Jesus face to face, as in Matthew, or sends messages to Jesus through representatives, as in Luke, one thing stands out in the story: the centurion's faith in the authority of Jesus. He is willing to take Jesus at his word.

Both Gospels highlight the faith of this Gentile. Matthew's Gospel is intent on the Jewishness of Jesus. His family tree in Matthew 1 traces the ancestry of Jesus back to Father Abraham and King David. He is called *Jesus the Messiah, the son of David, the son of Abraham.* Yet as early as Matthew 2 *wise men from the East* come to worship Jesus as *king of the Jews* and to give him *gold, frankincense, and myrrh*. Matthew's Gospel is also intent on the Gentile mission of the followers of Jesus. The Gentile centurion reminds Matthew's readers of the Gentile wise men who came seeking Jesus. It is true that about a third of the way through Matthew's Gospel Jesus restricts his twelve disciples' mission: *'Go nowhere among the Gentiles, and enter no town of the Samaritans, but go rather to the lost sheep of the house of Israel.' (Matthew 10:5)* But at the end of the Gospel Jesus the Jew gives his Jewish followers the Great Commission: *'All authority in heaven and on earth has been given to me. Go therefore and make disciples of all* nations.' (Matthew 28:18-19) Jesus has come first to the Jews and then to the Gentiles. That is to say, Jews and Gentiles are included in God's holy people. The Gentile centurion challenges Matthew's readers to look ahead to the worldwide mission of the church.

Luke's Gospel has a similar emphasis. As we read Luke's narrative we experience the reality of a ministry for all people. Jesus is trusted by downtrodden women, despised Samaritans, helpless poor, social outcasts, and even this Gentile centurion. According to Luke, the centurion has built the local synagogue, cares for his slave, is sensitive about asking a Jew to enter his Gentile home. His request comes through the elders of the synagogue and then his friends relay his faith in the power of Jesus. He recognises the authority of Jesus: *'But only speak the word, and let my servant be healed. For I also am a man set under authority ...'* He is a person of faith. As George Caird observes, 'Faith was to recognise that in Jesus the kingdom of God was exercising its power.'[2] The sequel to Luke in Acts 10 makes it explicit that the Gentile centurion in Capernaum is a forerunner to the Roman centurion in Caesarea. He is included in the programme of the risen Lord who commands his apostles: *'But you will receive power when the Holy Spirit has come upon you; and you will be my witnesses in Jerusalem, in all Judea and Samaria, and to the ends of the earth.' (Acts 1:8)*

Modern readers of this story will appreciate the gift of faith that God has given to people of all sorts and conditions. As someone who grew up in an Anglo Australian culture it is a real pleasure for me to go to church Sunday by Sunday and meet

---

[2] G.B. Caird, *Saint Luke*, p. 108.

followers of Jesus who are drawn from North and South Asia, from the Americas, from Europe, from Northern and Southern Africa. People from all over the world are still recognising the power and authority of God at work in Jesus the Lord. Modern Australia has come a long way from the White Australia Policy to the Multicultural Australia of today which includes refugees from the Wars in Vietnam, Iraq, Afghanistan, Syria, and Ukraine.

Reflection

Think about the faith of the centurion who submits to the authority of Jesus.

Prayer

Lord, help us to recognise the power and authority of God at work in the followers of Jesus, then in the Greco Roman world, and now in the entire world. Amen.

3 Peter's Mother-in-law

When Jesus entered Peter's house, he saw his mother-in-law lying in bed with a fever; he touched her hand, and the fever left her, and she got up and began to serve him. That evening they brought to him many who were possessed with demons; and he cast out the spirits with a word, and cured all who were sick. This was to fulfil what had been spoken through the prophet Isaiah, 'He took our infirmities and bore our diseases.'
(Matthew 8:14-17; compare Mark 1:29-34; Luke 4:38-41; Aland, *Synopsis* ## 37-38, 87-88)

Telling the Story

Capernaum's small houses from the first century included one room dwellings. Peter's house began this way but by the fourth century became the centre of a house church. Then an octagonal church was built in the fifth century around the house church. Sadly Arab invasion in the seventh century led to the destruction of the complex. I first saw the ruins in 1971. Its ruins were preserved in 1990 by the Franciscans who built an octagonal modern church over the ruins, with the modern church's floor being a suspended slab so that the ruins were still visible underneath. I saw the ruins again under this modern memorial in 2005. The veneration of the place before the fourth century allows us to assume that this really was the site of Peter's house in Capernaum.[1]

Matthew's story, the third in a row, tells of a particular case and then gives a general summary of Jesus' healing ministry. The particular case is the healing of Peter's mother-in-law. Jesus comes into Peter's house, sees Peter's mother-in-law lying in bed with a fever, and touches her hand. By this act, the fever

---

[1] See *Biblical Archaeology Review 200th Issue*, vol. 35 nos. 4/5, pp. 88-90.

leaves her and she gets up. The incident concludes with her starting to serve Jesus. Matthew's general summary of the evening follows with the cure of *many who were possessed with demons* and *all who were sick*. Matthew quotes Isaiah 53:4: *'He took our infirmities and bore our diseases.'*

Interpreting the Story

Matthew's account has three distinctive features. First, unlike Mark and Luke, Simon is called Peter. Is this in line with Matthew's developed version of Peter's confession of faith and the response of Jesus? *Simon Peter answered, 'You are the Messiah, the Son of the living God.' And Jesus answered him, 'Blessed are you, Simon son of Jonah! For flesh and blood has not revealed this to you, but my Father in heaven. And I tell you, you are Peter, and on this rock I will build my church, and the gates of Hades will not prevail against it. I will give you the keys of the kingdom of heaven, and whatever you bind on earth will be bound in heaven, and whatever you loose on earth will be loosed in heaven.' (Matthew 16:16-20)*

Second, Peter's mother-in-law gets up from her sick bed to serve Jesus. Whereas in Mark and Luke it is said that she served *them*, that is to say all the disciples, in Matthew it is said that she served *him*, that is to say Jesus. Is this an indication that serving others is serving Jesus?

Third, reference is made in Matthew's account to the oracles of Isaiah of Babylon as found in Isaiah 53:4-5. These verses were originally understood to be about redemptive suffering, *Surely he has borne our infirmities and carried our diseases ...But he was wounded for our transgressions, crushed for our iniquities.*

Matthew 8:17 interprets them as a reference to physical healing, *He took our infirmities and bore our diseases.* As Frank Stagg says, 'this passage may remind us that though the redeeming work of Christ has its center in the cross, he already was Redeemer from sickness and sin during his earthly ministry.'[2]

The record of Mark mentions the location as that of *the house of Simon and Andrew*, and includes *James and John* as eyewitnesses of the event. Mark's version of the summary of evening hearings refers to the impact of Jesus (*And the whole city was gathered around the door*) and concludes with the command of Jesus (*and he would not permit the demons to speak, because they knew him*). In Mark's Gospel the first eight chapters feature the Messianic Secret. Jesus does not want people to declare that he is Messiah. The last eight chapters explain the Messianic Suffering. Jesus wants people to know that being Messiah commits him to suffering and death ... and victory over death.

Luke's account is notable for its description of the sickness of Simon's mother-in-law in that it speaks of a high fever and of her cure after Jesus *stood over her and rebuked the fever, and it left her.* It is as though he is casting out with immediate effect an evil force. Luke concludes with an acknowledgement by demons (*'You are the Son of God!'*) and an explanation by Luke (*they knew that he was the Messiah.*) Greeks and Romans, and in this case powers of evil, were tempted to interpret Son of God in terms of a divine worker of wonders or an imperial ruler of a realm. However, the Gospel writers, including Luke,

---

[2] Frank Stagg, 'Matthew', *The Broadman Bible Commentary*, 8:126.

make it clear that Son of God is to be interpreted in terms of the Jewish Messiah who combines the roles of Servant of the Lord[3] and Son of Man.[4]

Experiencing the Story

Imagine that you are Simon Peter's mother-in-law and are known as the mother of a woman who is married to a man who will become known as the Big Fisherman. No longer is your daughter known by her mother but you are known by your daughter's husband. Helpless, you are now very sick. Where do you go for help? The surprising thing is that you don't have to go for help because help comes to you. As a result, you resume your role as an important member in your family.

It is true that mothers-in-law are not to be stereotyped in an unkind fashion. Indeed, there was a mother named Hazel who used to tell her churchgoing daughter that if she continued to go to church so much she would finish up marrying a minister. She did. However, Hazel became a very kind mother-in-law to her son-in-law. She was supportive of the achievements of both him and her daughter. With profound interest she followed the travels, the studies, the work and the growing family of the young couple.

There was also another mother whose name was Dorothy. Her talented daughter was advanced in her banking career. When her daughter met a widower with two young children, it was much to Dorothy's surprise that this 'career girl' was willing to

---

[3] See Isaiah 40-55, especially 53.

[4] See Daniel 7.

give up her career and marry the widower. Thus Dorothy now became mother-in-law to the widower and grandmother to his children. She found great joy in being an encouragement to this new 'instant family'.

After the account of the healings of Peter's mother-in-law and *many who were possessed with demons* and *all who were sick*, it is important to note the reference to the Old Testament. Matthew quotes Isaiah 53:4, *'He took our infirmities and bore our diseases.'* The Gospel writer is a positive example of the precept: 'Tell me what you find in the Bible, and I will tell you what you are.'[5] While the Bible may be misused by the legalist, it can also be utilised wisely.

As a very young Christian I learned to appreciate two biblical texts in the King James Bible. One was the promise of Romans 8:28, *And we know that all things work together for good to them that love God, to them who are the called according to his purpose.* The other was the benediction of Jude 24-25, *Now unto him that is able to keep you from falling, and to present you faultless before the presence of his glory with exceeding joy, To the only wise God our Saviour, be glory and majesty, dominion and power, both now and ever. Amen.* Down through the years the translations of the two texts have changed but the assurance of Romans 8:28 and the prayer of Jude 24-25 have enriched my life and work.

---

[5] Oskar Pfister cited by Wayne E. Oates, *The Bible in Pastoral Care*, p. 22.

Reflection

Think about the members of our families, some Christian and others not Christian.

Prayer

Lord, help us to treat our nearest and dearest with care and concern so that we may all grow to be people of faith, hope, and love. Amen.

4   A Gale

And when he got into the boat, his disciples followed him. A gale arose on the lake, so great that the boat was being swamped by the waves; but he was asleep. And they went and woke him up, saying, 'Lord, save us! We are perishing!' And he said to them, 'Why are you afraid, you of little faith?' Then he got up and rebuked the winds and the sea; and there was a dead calm. They were amazed, saying, 'What sort of man is this, that even the winds and the sea obey him?'
(Matthew 8:23-27; compare Mark 4:35-41; Luke 8:22-25; Aland, *Synopsis* ## 90, 136)

Telling the Story

Matthew's version of the stilling of the storm is told after Jesus discusses discipleship with possible followers. One had said, *'Teacher, I will follow you wherever you go.'* But Jesus reminded him of his wandering lifestyle. Another had asked for a delay before following Jesus. But Jesus had not allowed for such a delay. *'Follow me.'* According to Matthew, *when he got into the boat, his disciples followed him.* The underlying Greek is quite expressive and inserts *Behold!* before the report of *a gale* (or windstorm) that *arose on the lake.* The word translated *gale* is *seismos,* most commonly 'earthquake.'[1] Yet in the midst of this storm which swamps the boat, Matthew simply says, *but he* [Jesus] *was asleep.* However, in response to the disciples' plea, *'Lord, save us! We are perishing!'* Jesus wakes and asks, *'Why are you afraid, you of little faith?'* Then he gets up, rebukes the wind and the waves with a resulting *dead calm.* The disciples are astonished and say, *'What sort of man is this, that even the winds and the sea obey him?'* 'As in the healing

---

[1] Bauer et al., A *Greek-English Lexicon of the New Testament,* p. 918.

stories so here too: Jesus' power works its full effect immediately.'[2]

'Why are you afraid, you of little faith?'
Then he got up and rebuked the winds and the sea;
and there was a dead calm.

Interpreting the Story

Lake Galilee is 210 metres (689 feet) below sea level, 21 kilometres (13 miles) long, between 9 kilometres (5 1/2 miles) and 13 kilometres (8 miles) wide and as much as 49 metres (161 feet) deep. It has been suggested that Mark referred to the body of water as a sea rather than a lake to recall the Greek Old Testament's 'connotations of the sea as a chaotic and dangerous

---
[2] Dale C. Allison, Jr., *Matthew A Shorter Commentary*, p. 132.

force, that had now been mastered by Jesus.'[3] For example, the psalmist says to God: *You silence the roaring of the seas, the roaring of their waves*, and *You rule the raging of the sea; when its waves rise, you still them. (Psalm 65:7; 89:9)* Mark's version of the story is saying that what God did in Old Testament times is what Jesus is doing in his ministry and among his followers. As Mark's readers may well have faced Roman persecution, they are being assured that the power of the eternal Christ is greater than the power of the temporary Caesar.

Luke's account like Matthew's is a shorter version of Mark's. In Luke the disciples wake Jesus with the words, *'Master, Master, we are perishing!'* Jesus responds by rebuking *the wind and the raging waves* [literally *the wave of the water*]. The wind and waves *ceased, and there was a calm.* Jesus challenges the disciples, *'Where is your faith?'* They say, *'Who then is this, that he commands even the winds and the water, and they obey him?'* After the calming of the Galilean lake Luke tells the story of the calming of the confused man. One is again reminded of the psalmist's words, *You silence the roaring of the seas, the roaring of their waves,* **the tumult of the peoples.** *(Psalm 65:7)*

Interestingly, the wreck of a Galilean fishing boat was found in 1986 in the mud near Kibbutz Ginnosar by two brothers. Since then it has been restored and is now on display at the kibbutz. It dates from the period of Jesus' life and was capable of carrying

---

[3] Mark A. Chancey, 'Sea of Galilee', *The New Interpreter's Dictionary of the Bible*, 2:518.

fifteen people. It could be rowed or sailed.[4] This leads us back to Matthew's account. By tying the story of the stilling of the storm to the theme of following Jesus it may well be that Matthew interprets 'the journey of the disciples in the storm and the stilling of the storm with reference to discipleship, and that means with reference to the little ship of the Church.'[5]

Experiencing the Story

William Barclay, 'Willie', was the Church of Scotland preacher, teacher and author whose pulpit was a typewriter. His legacy was *The Daily Study Bible*, a scholarly yet popular commentary on the New Testament. He died in January 1978 at the age of 70. Clive Rawlins tells the story of Willie's life in a detailed biography. Chapter 15 'The Crucible of Suffering' is very compelling reading. It includes a section entitled 'In the Storms of Life'[6] and recounts the tragic death of Willie's nineteen year old daughter Barbara. She and her fiancé Billy accompanied by a twelve year old boy were drowned off the Irish coast when their yacht was caught in a storm. Willie suffered terribly. He referred to his daughter's death as 'the accidental destruction of the beautiful and the good.' His wife Kate suffered mentally, physically and spiritually.

---

[4] Shelley Wachsmann, 'The Galilee Boat - 2000 Year Old Hull Recovered Intact', *Biblical Archaeology Review,* vol. 14 no. 5, pp. 18-33.

[5] Günther Bornkamm, 'The Stilling of the Storm in Matthew', *Tradition and Interpretation in Matthew*, p. 55.

[6] Clive L. Rawlins, *William Barclay The Authorized Biography*, pp. 499-514.

Even so, Willie wrote a letter to a fellow author, Rita Snowden, in New Zealand and mentioned his response to the loss of his daughter. Part of the letter reads: 'We had the suspense of having to wait for three weeks until last Friday when Barbara's body was found. On Tuesday we had her funeral service. The service was a great relief. It marked the end of the chapter, but not as we who are Christian believe, the end of the book.'

Shortly afterwards Willie wrote his commentary on Matthew 8:23-27 in *The Daily Study Bible*. In his commentary Willie mentions 'the storms of life': 'the cold, bleak wind of sorrow,' 'the hot blast of passion,' and 'the storms of doubt.' Furthermore he says: 'The lesson of this story, the meaning of this story, the fact of this story is that when the storms of life shake our souls Jesus Christ is there; and in his presence the raging of the storm turns to the peace that no storm can ever take away.'

Reflection

Think about the storms of human life such as sorrow, passion, and doubt.

Prayer

Lord, when we are shaken by the storms of life assure us of your presence which brings us the peace that passes understanding. Amen.

5   A Paralysed Man

And after getting into a boat he crossed the water and came to his own town. And just then some people were carrying a paralysed man lying on a bed. When Jesus saw their faith, he said to the paralytic, 'Take heart, son; your sins are forgiven.' Then some of the scribes said to themselves, 'This man is blaspheming.' But Jesus, perceiving their thoughts, said, 'Why do you think evil in your hearts? For which is easier, to say, "Your sins are forgiven," or to say, "Stand up and walk"? But so that you may know that the Son of Man has authority on earth to forgive sins'—he then said to the paralytic—'Stand up, take your bed and go to your home.' And he stood up and went to his home. When the crowds saw it, they were filled with awe, and they glorified God, who had given such authority to human beings.
(Matthew 9:1-8; compare Mark 2:1-12; Luke 5:17-26; Aland, *Synopsis* ## 43, 92)

Telling the Story

Matthew abbreviates Mark's version. Jesus' *own town* is Capernaum, the headquarters of his early Galilean ministry, as we have seen, the location of Peter's house. Mark and Luke have more to say of the house. Matthew, like Mark and Luke, highlights that Jesus responds to *their faith*, the faith of the people who bring the paralysed man to Jesus. Jesus says, *'Take heart, son; your sins are forgiven.'* Jesus may be using the divine passive with the meaning: 'God has forgiven your sins', or he is claiming as *Son of Man* to be able to forgive sins. Either way, this raises the ire of *some of the scribes*, 'specialists in the law of Moses.'[1] Whereas forgiveness is unseen, healing can be seen, so Jesus says, *'Stand up, take your bed and go to your home.'* There is no way of gainsaying the impact of Jesus' words. *And he stood up and went to his home.* The onlookers are nonplussed. They are *filled with awe*. They give glory to

---

[1] Bauer et al., A *Greek-English Lexicon of the New Testament*, p. 206.

God because of the gift of *such authority to human beings*. The reference here to the Son of Man recalls the visions of Daniel concerning the judge at the end of time. *I saw one like a human being* [Aramaic, *one like a son of man*] *coming with the clouds of heaven. And he came to the Ancient One* [Aramaic, *the Ancient of Days*] *and was presented before him. To him was given dominion and glory and kingship, that all peoples, nations, and languages should serve him. (Daniel 7:13-14)* In the midst of the ministry of Jesus the Son of Man, God's work of forgiveness and healing is already taking place and in the ongoing work of the followers of Jesus, that work continues.

'Stand up, take your bed and go to your home.'
And he stood up and went to his home.

Interpreting the Story

Mark gives a fulsome description of the efforts of the four friends of the paralysed man as they dig through a typical Galilean mud roof. *And when they could not bring him to Jesus because of the crowd, they removed the roof above him; and after having dug through it, they let down the mat on which the paralytic lay.* On the other hand, Luke says, *but finding no way to bring him in because of the crowd, they went up on the roof and let him down with his bed through the tiles into the middle of the crowd in front of Jesus.* Luke is writing about men who remove tiles from a typical Roman tiled roof. Among the spectators Luke mentions *Pharisees and teachers of the law.* This may indicate a single group. 'It was the purpose of the **Pharisees** to take the pattern of a pious Israelite established by the **scribes**, and to put it into practice as nearly as possible.'[2] In the face of such opposition Jesus honours the faith which is measured not by propositional precision but by personal persistence. Finally, in Mark the crowd says, *'We have never seen anything like this!'* In Luke they say, *'We have seen strange things today.'* The combination of forgiveness and healing points to the significance of Jesus.

Experiencing the Story

Some scholars think that the original version in Mark is a fusion of two incidents, one a miracle story about a healing and the other a pronouncement story about forgiveness. However, it is quite possible to accept the originality of a story about both healing and forgiveness. In modern times people have experienced healing and forgiveness together.

For example, there is the case of a woman with a blood deficiency.[3] A doctor referred her to a district medical officer

---

[2] Ibid., p. 1049.

[3] Paul Tournier cited by William Barclay, *The Daily Study Bible: Matthew*, 1:327-328.

for permission to spend time in a sanatorium. The officer gave her a permit but told the doctor that his analysis of the patient's blood revealed no deficiency. The doctor then took another blood sample for testing. Sure enough, her blood count had changed for the better. The doctor was certain that he had not made a mistake. When the doctor next saw the woman he asked her if something extraordinary had happened since her last visit. She told him that she had suddenly been able to let go of a horrible grudge and forgive the person involved. As a result she felt relieved and free. Here was the explanation of the improvement in her blood: a healthy mind in a healthy body.

The combination of healing of sickness and forgiveness of sin is in accord 'with the Hebrew view of the human being as a psychosomatic unity, an indivisible amalgam of body and soul in which if either goes wrong, the other is affected.'[4]

Reflection

Think about times in which healing and forgiveness have been needed.

Prayer

Lord, have mercy on people who need your healing touch and forgiving word. Make us your instruments of healing and forgiving peace. Amen.

---

[4] Frederick Buechner, *Beyond Words*, pp. 145-146.

6   A Woman and a Girl

While he was saying these things to them, suddenly a leader of the synagogue came in and knelt before him, saying, 'My daughter has just died; but come and lay your hand on her, and she will live.' And Jesus got up and followed him, with his disciples. Then suddenly a woman who had been suffering from haemorrhages for twelve years came up behind him and touched the fringe of his cloak, for she said to herself, 'If I only touch his cloak, I will be made well.' Jesus turned, and seeing her he said, 'Take heart, daughter; your faith has made you well.' And instantly the woman was made well. When Jesus came to the leader's house and saw the flute players and the crowd making a commotion, he said, 'Go away; for the girl is not dead but sleeping.' And they laughed at him. But when the crowd had been put outside, he went in and took her by the hand, and the girl got up. And the report of this spread throughout that district.
(Matthew 9:18-26; compare Mark 5:21-43; Luke 8:40-56; Aland, *Synopsis* ## 95, 138)

Telling the Story

Matthew's version is but a summary of Mark's. According to Matthew, *suddenly* [literally *behold*] *a leader of the synagogue came in and knelt before* Jesus. The leader then pleads, *'My daughter has just died; but come and lay your hand on her, and she will live.'*

On his way to help, *suddenly* [literally *behold*] Jesus encounters *a woman who had been suffering from haemorrhages for twelve years.* In other words, she is considered unclean in the Mosaic Law, which reads, *If a woman has a discharge of blood for many days ... all the days of the discharge she shall continue in uncleanness. (Leviticus 15:25)* Isolated and desperate, the woman says to herself, *'If I only touch* [the fringe of] *his cloak, I will be made well.'* The fringe of the cloak is mentioned in the Mosaic Law: *Tell them to make fringes on the corners of their garments throughout*

32

their generations ... You have the fringe so that, when you see it, you will remember all the commandments of the LORD and do them ... (Numbers 15:37-39) When the woman touches the fringe, Jesus turns and responds, *'Take heart, daughter; your faith has made you well.'* From that hour the woman is made well.

The narrative reverts to the plight of the young girl. To the mourners at the leader's house Jesus says, *'Go away; for the girl is not dead but sleeping.'* With the crowd outside, Jesus *took her by the hand, and the girl got up.*

In Matthew's account there are three parallels. First, the leader pleads for his *daughter* and Jesus calls the neglected woman *daughter.* Jesus is compassionate to the leader's daughter and to the suffering woman. Second, the woman wants to touch Jesus' cloak, which she does, and the leader wants Jesus to lay his hand on his daughter, which he does. The power of Jesus is at work in both cases. Third, the leader believes that his daughter *will live* and the woman believes that she *will be made well.* The faith of the leader and the woman is directed towards Jesus. He does not let them down.

Interpreting the Story

Mark and Luke include other interesting details. Both give the name of the leader of the synagogue. The Greek *Jairus* may be related to the Hebrew *Jair* used of names in the Old Testament meaning 'he enlightens' or 'he arouses'.[1] Mark calls the girl his

---

[1] Bauer et al., A *Greek-English Lexicon of the New Testament*, p. 464.

little daughter, while Luke says that she is his *only daughter, about twelve years old*.

Turning to the woman, Mark says that *she had endured much under many physicians, and had spent all that she had; and she was no better, but rather grew worse*. Luke, on the other hand, says *though she had spent all she had on physicians, no one could cure her.* (Does Luke, *the beloved physician (Colossians 4:14)*, soften the reference to physicians for professional reasons!?) Both Gospels mention the power of Jesus to heal. In Mark Jesus is *immediately aware that power had gone forth from him* and he says, *'Who touched my clothes?'* In Luke Jesus says, *'Someone touched me; for I noticed that power had gone out from me.'* Both Gospels also mention the gift of peace. In Mark and Luke Jesus says, *'Daughter, your faith has made you well; go in peace, and be healed of your disease.'*

Returning to the girl in Mark, Jesus reassures the leader, *'Do not fear, only believe.'* Jesus also challenges the crowd, *'Why do you make a commotion and weep? The child is not dead but sleeping.'* In private Jesus addresses the girl in Aramaic, *'Talitha cum,'* which means, *'Little girl, get up!'*[2] Mark concludes with a reference to her recovery, her age, and her need to eat. Luke follows and abbreviates Mark.

Experiencing the Story

If we imagine that we are part of one of these linked stories, we shall probably sense the power of Jesus felt by the people involved.

[2] Ibid., pp. 988, 563.

First, the woman is caught in an unenviable situation. She is suffering terribly and is on her own. She has sought help and has not found it. She is akin to people we know, if we are not such a one ourselves. What are her options? Does she continue to suffer in silence? Does she try to find help again? Does she dare to trust this man from Galilee? She interrupts him on his way to a local leader's home. She is saying to herself, *'If I only touch* [the fringe of] *his cloak, I will be made well* [literally *saved*].' When she does so, she amazingly feels different. According to Mark, *immediately her haemorrhage stopped; and she felt in her body that she was healed of her disease.* What does Jesus do? Does he ignore her? No! Rather, following Mark's account, he is *immediately aware that power had gone forth from him*, and he asks, *'Who touched my clothes?'* The woman, knowing the change in herself, comes *in fear and trembling*, kneels before him, and tells him *the whole truth*. Jesus says to her, *'Daughter, your faith has made you well* [literally *saved*]; *go in peace, and be healed of your disease.'* As Alan Culpepper says, 'She has been made whole in body and spirit by her encounter with Jesus.'[3] In what ways do we identify with the woman?

Second, the father of the girl is worried sick. The Gospels may differ but the situation is grim. According to Mark, the father begs Jesus repeatedly, *'My little daughter is at the point of death.'* In Matthew he says, *'My daughter has just died.'* Luke reports that *she was dying*. What can the father do? Has he heard of this man from Nazareth? Does he recall the promise of the prophet? *Your dead shall live, their corpses shall rise.*

---
[3] R. Alan Culpepper, *Mark*, p. 176.

(Isaiah 26:19) Will he choose fear or faith? If he chooses fear of the power of death, all is lost. If he chooses faith in the power of Jesus, all is in the hand of God. Mark and Luke report that as the leader goes to his home Jesus says to him, *'Do not fear, only believe.'*

The command not to fear or be afraid echoes throughout the Bible. The following examples will suffice: *'Do not fear or be dismayed.' (Deuteronomy 1:21; Joshua 8:1) With the LORD on my side I do not fear. (Psalm 118:6) Say to those who are of a fearful heart, 'Be strong, do not fear!' (Isaiah 35:6) Do not fear, for I am with you, do not be afraid, for I am your God. (Isaiah 41:10)* It is fitting that Jesus says, *'Do not fear, only believe.'* Jairus, a fearful father who is afraid that his daughter is in the grip of death, learns to trust. As Frederick Buechner observes, 'Faith is better understood as a verb than as a noun, as a process than as a possession.'[4]

Reflection

Think about people we have known who have helped and guided us along the path of life.

Prayer

Lord, we thank you for the example of the woman in an unenviable situation who trusted in Jesus and of the father who was worried sick but chose faith over fear. Amen.

---

[4] Frederick Buechner, *Beyond Words*, p. 109.

Part 2: Miracles in Mark's Gospel

A Prayer for Readers of Mark's Gospel[1]

Living God of Mark's Good News about Jesus, we thank you for Jesus, the bounding lion and the heroic leader. Fill us with the lion's boundless energy and guide us by this leader's purposeful direction. Let us be faithful and fearless in word and deed as we seek to follow Jesus. Amen.

---

[1] Doug Rowston, *A Bird's Eye View of the Bible Second Edition*, p. 131.

7   A Gerasene Demoniac

They came to the other side of the lake to the country of the Gerasenes. And when he had stepped out of the boat, immediately a man out of the tombs with an unclean spirit met him. He lived among the tombs; and no one could restrain him any more, even with a chain; for he had often been restrained with shackles and chains, but the chains he wrenched apart, and the shackles he broke in pieces; and no one had the strength to subdue him. Night and day among the tombs and on the mountains he was always howling and bruising himself with stones. When he saw Jesus from a distance, he ran and bowed down before him; and he shouted at the top of his voice, 'What have you to do with me, Jesus, Son of the Most High God? I adjure you by God, do not torment me.' For he had said to him, 'Come out of the man, you unclean spirit!' Then Jesus asked him, 'What is your name?' He replied, 'My name is Legion; for we are many.' He begged him earnestly not to send them out of the country. Now there on the hillside a great herd of swine was feeding; and the unclean spirits begged him, 'Send us into the swine; let us enter them.' So he gave them permission. And the unclean spirits came out and entered the swine; and the herd, numbering about two thousand, rushed down the steep bank into the lake, and were drowned in the lake. The swineherds ran off and told it in the city and in the country. Then people came to see what it was that had happened. They came to Jesus and saw the demoniac sitting there, clothed and in his right mind, the very man who had had the legion; and they were afraid. Those who had seen what had happened to the demoniac and to the swine reported it. Then they began to beg Jesus to leave their neighbourhood. As he was getting into the boat, the man who had been possessed by demons begged him that he might be with him. But Jesus refused, and said to him, 'Go home to your friends, and tell them how much the Lord has done for you, and what mercy he has shown you.' And he went away and began to proclaim in the Decapolis how much Jesus had done for him; and everyone was amazed.
(Mark 5:1-20; compare Matthew 8:28-34; Luke 8:26-39; Aland, *Synopsis* # 91)

Telling the Story

As Vincent Taylor points out, Mark tells the story in four stages.[1] First, interest is directed towards *a man out of the*

---

[1] Vincent Taylor, *The Gospel According To St. Mark*, p. 277.

tombs with an unclean spirit. He is incapable of restraint, *even with shackles and chains,* and *among the tombs and on the mountains* he is *always howling and bruising himself.* When he encounters Jesus, the sad and lonely man says, *'What have you to do with me, Jesus, Son of the Most High God? I adjure you by God, do not torment me.'* This is in response to Jesus who had ordered, *'Come out of the man, you unclean spirit!'* Jesus asks the demon possessed man, *'What is your name?'* The troubled man replies, *'My name is Legion; for we are many.'* At the mercy of demonic forces the man identifies himself with a legion of evil spirits and requests that they should not be sent out of the country. The Roman army was numbered in legions, units of about 6000 soldiers.² Perhaps we could say that the man is suffering from a split personality. At any rate, as Vincent Taylor says of another exorcism, 'Jesus shares the ideas of his time, but so far transcends them that by a commanding word alone, without the use of magical practices, He casts out the unclean spirit. He Himself is the subject of the story.'³

Second, attention turns to an unlikely subject: *a great herd of swine.* Of course, swine or pigs are unclean animals according to Leviticus 11:7-8, *The pig, for even though it has divided hoofs and is cleft-footed, it does not chew the cud; it is unclean for you. Of their flesh you shall not eat, and their carcasses you shall not touch; they are unclean for you.* It is probable that the region is populated by Gentiles who have no qualms about Jewish laws. The unclean spirits beg Jesus, *'Send us into the swine; let us enter them.'* Subsequently the herd of two thousand pigs rushes down the steep bank into the lake, and are

---

² Bauer et al., A *Greek-English Lexicon of the New Testament,* p. 588.

³ Vincent Taylor, *The Gospel According To St. Mark,* p. 171.

drowned in the lake. Unclean spirits are destroyed with unclean animals.

Third, informed by the swineherds, the people from the nearby town and country come to see what has happened. They find the transformed man *sitting there, clothed and in his right mind*. This is the same man who had been demon possessed, but he is not the same. The town and country people are afraid. Even though witnesses have seen what happened, fearful people begin to beg Jesus to go away from their neighbourhood.

Fourth, interest is redirected to *the man who had been possessed by demons*, who begs Jesus to allow him to accompany him. But Jesus refuses saying, *'Go home to your friends, and tell them how much the Lord has done for you, and what mercy he has shown you.'* The man goes away and begins to proclaim in the Gentile Ten Towns how much Jesus has done for him. As Vincent Taylor notes, 'The man is commanded to tell what God had done for him, but instead he tells of the work of Jesus.'[4] No wonder that everyone is amazed.

Interpreting the Story

In interpreting the story, one may note the differing locations in the three Gospels: the country of the Gerasenes (Mark and Luke), the Gadarenes (Matthew), and the Gergasenes (a variant reading suggested by other ancient authorities). The first is Geresa fifty nine kilometres (thirty seven miles) south east of Lake Galilee. The second is Gadara eight kilometres (five

---

[4] Ibid., p. 285.

miles) south east of Lake Galilee. The third is Gergesa on the eastern shore. Leslie Hoppe says, 'Neither study of the textual variants nor the results of excavation has been successful in identifying the setting for the exorcism narrated in the Synoptics.'[5]

Luke agreeing with Mark speaks of *a man of the city who had demons*, who wears no clothes and does not live *in a house but in the tombs*, whereas Matthew's version of the story features *two demoniacs coming out of the tombs*. Perhaps Matthew tells of two demoniacs[6] in Matthew 8:28-34, in accord with an Old Testament dictum: *Only on the evidence of two or three witnesses shall a charge be sustained. (Deuteronomy 19:15)*

Mark emphasises the change in the man: *sitting there, clothed and in his right mind*. But Matthew stresses two things. Jesus defeats the demons, who recognise him as *'Son of God'* and then beg him, *'If you cast us out, send us into the herd of swine.'* The swineherds and townspeople choose fear rather than faith. *The swineherds ... told the whole story ... Then the whole town ... begged him to leave their neighbourhood.*

Luke's account highlights the words of Jesus to the changed man, *'Return to your home, and declare how much God has done for you.'* The man goes away, *proclaiming throughout the city how much Jesus had done for him*. As Howard Marshall

---

[5] Leslie J. Hoppe, 'Gerasa, Gerasenes', *The New Interpreter's Dictionary of the Bible*, 2:557. Compare the map in R. Alan Culpepper, *Mark*, p. 165 for the locations of the three sites.

[6] Matthew also tells of the healing of two blind men (9:27-31) and two other blind men (20:29-34).

says, 'The story is a paradigm of what conversion involves: the responsibility to evangelise.'[7]

Experiencing the Story

Despite its strangeness, this story of Jesus expelling demons remains relevant to a world in which people feel at the mercy of hostile forces. Representatives of Jesus whether they be lay or clergy have the privilege and responsibility to bring the light of God into dark places. As Alan Culpepper says, 'Mark 5:1-20 is a story that may give hope to many as they struggle with family members who have been overcome by alcoholism, drug addiction, depression, or mental illness.'[8]

Things have changed in institutions for the mentally ill in the last fifty years but the following account still carries a message of hope. Walter Jackson was a student chaplain in a large mental hospital outside Louisville, Kentucky about sixty years ago. He attended a worship service including more than 450 patients at the hospital. The senior chaplain gave a call to worship from the Bible but he was interrupted by a very disturbed, poorly dressed middle aged woman patient. She stood up, pointed her finger at him, and shouted, 'Go to Hell!' There was silence. She repeated her curse twice. Silence ensued until an older and similarly dressed woman patient shouted and pointed her finger at the first woman saying, 'Shut

---

[7] I. Howard Marshall, *The Gospel of Luke*, p. 341.

[8] R. Alan Culpepper, *Mark*, p. 181.

up and sit down; we're already there! This good chaplain has come to help us get out!'[9]

About a decade after that worship service I completed a unit in Clinical Pastoral Education at the same hospital. As a student chaplain I had responsibility for two wards of about a dozen patients each. No longer were the patients gathered in such a large group together for worship services. Instead, weekly services were held by a chaplain on each ward. Even so, disturbed patients would interrupt occasionally. It was still the task of a chaplain to point patients in the direction of Jesus.

Reflection

Think about the causes and effects of deeply disturbed people in our society.

Prayer

Lord, you are the one who lifts us out of despair into hope, out of desperation into joy. Help us and those for whom we pray to know such a transition. Amen.

---

[9] Walter C. Jackson, 'A Brief History of Theological Education including a Description of the Contribution of Wayne E. Oates', *Review and Expositor*, 94:518, 1997.

8 A Syrophoenician Woman

From there he set out and went away to the region of Tyre. He entered a house and did not want anyone to know he was there. Yet he could not escape notice, but a woman whose little daughter had an unclean spirit immediately heard about him, and she came and bowed down at his feet. Now the woman was a Gentile, of Syrophoenician origin. She begged him to cast the demon out of her daughter. He said to her, 'Let the children be fed first, for it is not fair to take the children's food and throw it to the dogs.' But she answered him, 'Sir, even the dogs under the table eat the children's crumbs.' Then he said to her, 'For saying that, you may go—the demon has left your daughter.' So she went home, found the child lying on the bed, and the demon gone.
(Mark 7:24-30; compare Matthew 15:21-28; Aland, *Synopsis* # 151)

Telling the Story

In *the region of Tyre* north-west of Galilee on the Mediterranean coast Jesus is seeking some privacy. However, he does not escape attention in this Gentile territory. A woman whose *little daughter* has *an unclean spirit* comes, falls in front of him, and begs him to expel *the demon* from the girl. The woman is *a Gentile* [literally *Greek*], *of Syrophoenician origin*. Vincent Taylor notes, 'Mark ... describes the woman by her religion and her nationality.'[1] Jesus responds to her request, *'Let the children be fed first, for it is not fair to take the children's food* [literally *bread*] *and throw it to the dogs.'* Is Jesus contrasting the Jews (*the children*) with the Gentiles (*the dogs*)? Jesus' answer may not be harsh. The underlying Greek for dogs refers to 'a house-dog or lap-dog in contrast to a dog of the street or farm.'[2] The woman answers, *'Sir* [literally *Lord*], *even the dogs under the table eat the children's crumbs.'*

---

[1] Vincent Taylor, *The Gospel According To St. Mark*, p. 349.

[2] Bauer et al., A *Greek-English Lexicon of the New Testament*, p. 575.

As Taylor comments, 'Jesus is pleased by the woman's wit and persistence.'[3] Jesus tells the woman, *'For saying that, you may go—the demon has left your daughter.'* Going home she finds the child lying in bed with the demon gone.

Interpreting the Story

Locating the incident in *the district of Tyre and Sidon*, Matthew identifies the mother as *a Canaanite woman*. She starts shouting, *'Have mercy on me, Lord, Son of David; my daughter is tormented by a demon.'* After not answering her at all, Jesus is approached by his disciples who say, *'Send her away, for she keeps shouting after us.'* He answers the disciples, *'I was sent only to the lost sheep of the house of Israel.'* The woman apparently overhears, will not give up, and says, *'Lord, help me.'* Matthew then follows Mark. Jesus says, *'It is not fair to take the children's food and throw it to the dogs.'* The woman replies, *'Yes, Lord, yet even the dogs eat the crumbs that fall from their masters' table.'* Matthew highlights her faith. Jesus says, *'Woman, great is your faith! Let it be done for you as you wish.'* According to Matthew, the daughter is healed *instantly* [literally *from that hour*].

Unlike Mark, Matthew's account speaks of the woman as *a Canaanite*. In the Old Testament Canaanites were the inhabitants of the promised land before the entry of Joshua and the Israelites. Matthew is probably inferring that, as a non-Jewess she is religiously unclean. Surprisingly, she addresses Jesus as *Lord* three times and as *Son of David* once. Jesus' reference to his sole mission *to the lost sheep of the house of*

---

[3] Vincent Taylor, *The Gospel According To St. Mark*, p. 351.

Israel does not deter her; she asks for help. But Jesus talks about *the children's food* and *the dogs*. Even so, the woman refers to *the dogs* and *the crumbs*! Her faith is rewarded and the young girl is healed.

Frank Stagg observes that there are three possible interpretations of the matter of Jesus' reaction to the Canaanite woman in Matthew.[4] First, is he testing the woman's faith? Probably not. Second, is he instructing the disciples in view of their impatience? Possibly so. Third, is Jesus struggling with turning from Jews to Gentiles at this stage of his ministry? Earlier he had said, *'Go nowhere among the Gentiles, and enter no town of the Samaritans, but go rather to the lost sheep of the house of Israel.' (Matthew 10:5-6)* Later he would say, *'Go therefore and make disciples of all nations, baptizing them in the name of the Father and of the Son and of the Holy Spirit, and teaching them to obey everything that I have commanded you.' (Matthew 28:19-20)* One thinks of the Apostle Paul's thesis, *The gospel ... is the power of God for salvation to everyone who has faith, to the Jew first and also to the Greek. (Romans 1:16)* Tom Long suggests, 'This story mirrors the development that Matthew's church itself was perhaps experiencing - from a silent separation from Gentiles, to an annoyed awareness of their presence, and ultimately to an active Gentile mission.'[5]

---

[4] Frank Stagg, 'Matthew', *The Broadman Bible Commentary*, 8:168-169.

[5] Thomas G. Long, *Matthew*, p. 177.

Experiencing the Story

The care of Jesus for the Canaanite or Syrophoenician woman brings to mind the care of Ida Scudder for neglected women in South India.[6] In 1890 young Ida was visiting her missionary parents. Overnight she was asked to help three Muslim women who were about to give birth but, being untrained medically, Ida could not do so. Due to local custom, each of the women's husbands would not allow their wives to be treated by a male doctor. In the morning Ida was horrified to learn that each woman had died. She felt that God was calling her to ministry among the women and children of India.

She returned to the United States and commenced medical training. In 1899 she became one of the first women to graduate from Cornell Medical College, New York City. Going back to India in 1900, Ida opened a clinic with one bed in Vellore. After two years there were forty beds for patients. She established a school of nursing in 1909 and a medical school for women in 1918. In 1942 it became a medical college which, after 1947, also catered for men. Such were the origins of the Christian Medical College and Hospital with 1800 beds today. It owes its existence to the vision of Ida Sophia Scudder (1870-1960) who chose its motto, 'Not to be ministered unto, but to minister' (Mark 10:45 KJV). In her case, the persistence of one blessed woman led to the blessing of the underprivileged and previously unblessed.

---

[6] http://australianfov.net.au; https://cfmedicine.nlm.nih.gov/physicians/biography_290.html; https://en.wikipedia.org/wiki/Ida_S._Scudder

Reflection

Think about the neglected men, women and children in both our country and beyond our shores.

Prayer

Lord, raise our awareness of the existence of the needs of the neglected and enable us to contribute personally and collectively to the well being of those known to us. Amen.

9   A Deaf and Dumb Man

Then he returned from the region of Tyre, and went by way of Sidon towards the Sea of Galilee, in the region of the Decapolis. They brought to him a deaf man who had an impediment in his speech; and they begged him to lay his hand on him. He took him aside in private, away from the crowd, and put his fingers into his ears, and he spat and touched his tongue. Then looking up to heaven, he sighed and said to him, 'Ephphatha,' that is, 'Be opened.' And immediately his ears were opened, his tongue was released [literally *the bond of his tongue was loosed*], *and he spoke plainly. Then Jesus ordered them to tell no one; but the more he ordered them, the more zealously they proclaimed it. They were astounded beyond measure, saying, 'He has done everything well; he even makes the deaf to hear and the mute to speak.'*
(Mark 7:31-37; Aland, *Synopsis* # 152)

Telling the Story

According to Mark, Jesus returns *from the region of Tyre,* and goes *by way of Sidon towards the Sea of Galilee, in the region of the Decapolis.* The geography is interesting, to say the least. As Vincent Taylor says, 'The route described is circuitous and uncertain.'[1] The story has Jesus going north to Sidon, southeast past Caesarea Philippi to Lake Galilee, then east through the Decapolis (the Ten Towns).[2] The commentators ask if the author of Mark is conversant with the region or if he is simply describing a roundabout route which may have taken a while.

However, the focus is *a deaf man who* has *an impediment in his speech*. 'Speaking with difficulty, having an impediment in one's speech' and 'mute, unable to articulate' are both possible

---

[1] Vincent Taylor, *The Gospel According To St. Mark*, p. 352.

[2] See the map in Pheme Perkins, 'The Gospel of Mark', *The New Interpreter's Bible*, 8:610.

translations of the underlying Greek.[3] Isaiah, the Old Testament prophet, had promised, *'Then the eyes of the blind shall be opened, and the ears of the deaf unstopped; then the lame shall leap like a deer, and the tongue of the speechless sing for joy.' (Isaiah 35:5-6)* Jesus is asked to lay a hand on him. He takes the deaf mute aside. Jesus puts his fingers in the man's ears, spits on his own hands, and touches the man's tongue. As Alan Culpepper observes, Jesus is acting out the opening of the man's ears and is applying spittle from a free tongue to a bound tongue.[4] Next he looks up *to heaven*, and sighing, says in Aramaic, *'Ephphatha,'* which means, *'Be opened.' Immediately*[5] the man's ears are opened, his tongue is released, and he speaks plainly.

Although Jesus orders them not to tell anyone, the more he orders, the more they do tell everyone. Indeed, the onlookers are astonished saying, *'He has done everything well; he even makes the deaf to hear and the mute to speak.'* The first clause recalls the words of the first creation story, *God saw everything that he had made, and indeed, it was very good. (Genesis 1:31)* The second clause basically says that Jesus is fulfilling the promise of Isaiah, *The eyes of the blind shall be opened, and the ears of the deaf unstopped. (Isaiah 35:5)*

---

[3] Bauer et al., A *Greek-English Lexicon of the New Testament*, p. 656.

[4] R. Alan Culpepper, *Mark*, p. 245.

[5] The Greek word *euthys* translated 'immediately', 'at once', 'shortly', 'so then' occurs 41 times in Mark. (Vincent Taylor, *The Gospel According To St. Mark*, p. 160.)

Interpreting the Story

The healing of this deaf and dumb man is only told in Mark, although Matthew 15:30-31 is a generalised account in which Jesus cures many people. As a result, *the crowd was amazed when they saw the mute speaking, the maimed whole, the lame walking, and the blind seeing. And they praised the God of Israel.* Why is Mark the only evangelist to tell the story? Perhaps Matthew and Luke avoid repeating the story because of such strange features as Jesus putting his fingers in the man's ears, spitting on his own hands, touching the man's tongue, looking up to heaven, sighing and groaning, and speaking in Aramaic. Do Matthew and Luke wish to avoid the suggestion that Jesus is a magician? Jesus does not manipulate the divine, but he does reveal the divine dominion. Matthew and Luke are agreed that Jesus answered John the Baptist's question about Jesus' identity by saying, *'Go and tell John what you hear and see: the blind receive their sight, the lame walk, the lepers are cleansed, the deaf hear, the dead are raised, and the poor have good news brought to them. And blessed is anyone who takes no offence at me.' (Matthew 11:4-6; compare Luke 7:22-23)*

Experiencing the Story

First, let us imagine that we are afflicted by poor hearing. This has become an issue for me personally. A year or so ago I found that I had to hold a telephone to my left ear because I could hear nothing using my right ear. The telephone which did not work in the right ear suddenly became effective on the other side! Of course, auditory tests revealed a huge discrepancy between right and left ears and my right ear is now the depository of a highly expensive hearing aid.

As Frederick Buechner notes, 'A deaf man coming upon me listening to you would think that nothing of importance was going on. But something of extraordinary importance is going on ... Hearing you speak brings me by the most direct of all routes something of the innermost secret of who you are.' Hearing is important in the Old Testament. We read more than 400 times, 'Thus says the LORD'. Accordingly Buechner continues, 'It is no surprise that the Bible uses hearing, not seeing, as the predominant image for the way human beings know God.'[6] The story of the healing of the **deaf** and dumb man challenges us to move from poor listening to attentive listening when it comes to the stories of Jesus.

Second, let us imagine that we are afflicted by inarticulate speaking. This can become an issue for someone whose speaking facility is affected by debilitating disease or advancing age. We may encounter people whose ability to speak or sing is diminished by a throat operation which affects the vocal cords. And then there are people whose ageing process results in garbled speech.

The spoken word is, for good or ill, a significant force. As Frederick Buechner writes, 'Words are power, essentially the power of creation. By my words I both discover and create who I am. By my words I elicit a word from you. Through our converse we create each other.'[7] If hearing is important in the

---

[6] Frederick Buechner, *Beyond Words*, p. 148.

[7] Ibid., p. 413.

Bible, so is speaking. God speaks to human beings and believers are meant to speak for God in word and deed. We are like teachers who having heard and read our subjects, gain basic understanding. Then by teaching our subjects through speaking and writing, we experience deeper understanding. The story of the healing of the deaf and **dumb** man challenges us to move from inarticulate speaking to effective speaking in communicating the message of Jesus.

Reflection

Think about the needs of people who suffer impaired hearing and garbled speech.

Prayer

Lord, give us sensitivity when we encounter a deaf or dumb person. If we happen to suffer such an impediment, give us patience. Amen.

10   A Blind Man

They came to Bethsaida. Some people brought a blind man to him and begged him to touch him. He took the blind man by the hand and led him out of the village; and when he had put saliva on his eyes and laid his hands on him, he asked him, 'Can you see anything?' And the man looked up and said, 'I can see people, but they look like trees, walking.' Then Jesus laid his hands on his eyes again; and he looked intently and his sight was restored, and he saw everything clearly. Then he sent him away to his home, saying, 'Do not even go into the village.'
(Mark 8:22-26; Aland, *Synopsis* # 156)

Telling the Story

At *Bethsaida*, east of the River Jordan and north of Lake Galilee,[1] some people bring a blind man to Jesus and beg Jesus to touch him. Taking him by the hand, Jesus leads him out of the village. Then the NRSV translates delicately *when he had put saliva on his eyes and laid his hands on him*. The Greek is literally *having spat (or spit) into his eyes, having laid the hands on him*. Subsequently Jesus asks the blind man if he can see anything. The man looks up and says, *'I can see people, but they look like trees, walking.'* In Greek his answer is literally, *'I see people, but I perceive (them or something) as trees walking.'* Jesus again lays his hands on the man's eyes. The man looks intently, is cured and sees all things clearly in the distance. As Vincent Taylor says, 'The second laying on of hands implies that the first was not successful and that the cure was gradual.'[2] Jesus sends the healed man away to his home saying, *'Do not even go into the village.'*

---

[1] See the map in R. Alan Culpepper, *Mark*, p. 264.

[2] Vincent Taylor, *The Gospel According To St. Mark*, p. 372.

Interpreting the Story

Why is Mark the only evangelist to tell the story of the blind man? Perhaps Matthew and Luke avoid repeating the story because of strange features like Jesus spitting in the man's eyes, laying his hands on the man's eyes a second time. As Ben Witherington says, 'In a world of instant everything, not all good things can be had immediately, especially when we are talking about healing. Even Jesus didn't always produce instant miracles on demand.'[3] Perhaps Matthew and Luke again wish to avoid the suggestion that Jesus is a magician. Mark would insist that Jesus does not manipulate the divine, he inaugurates the divine dominion.

Mark tells two parallel stories of a deaf and dumb man in Mark 7:31-37 and a blind man in Mark 8:22-26. As Alan Culpepper says, 'Taken together these two miracle accounts affirm that Jesus fulfilled the expectations of Isaiah 35:5-6, that the Messiah would give hearing to the deaf and sight to the blind.'[4]

Experiencing the Story

Culpepper wisely observes, 'Like the blind man we need Jesus' second touch. Unlike the blind man, that second touch usually does not come immediately.'[5]

---

[3] Ben Witherington III, *The Gospel of Mark*, p. 252.

[4] R. Alan Culpepper, *Mark*, p. 244.

[5] Ibid., p. 284.

The life of Wayne Oates illustrates this remark.6 In 1932, as a poor and fatherless fifteen year old in a South Carolina church youth group, he was intrigued by a remark of the leader, a ministerial student from a nearby university. Wayne had been asked to say a prayer, which he did. Afterwards the ministerial student had observed, 'His prayers didn't get any higher than the ceiling because he is not baptised.' In fact, Wayne had been engaged in personal prayer and was aware of God's presence since the age of four. This had nothing to do with churchgoing and praying publicly.

Soon after the disparaging incident the pastor's wife at that church approached Wayne about becoming a Christian. He said that he would like to and in a short time he professed his faith in Christ, was baptised by immersion at the time of his sixteenth birthday. However, he received no instruction about being a Christian, only instruction about giving a tithe of his income, and Wayne's income was very little! So much for the first touch of the Master on his life! Providentially, Wayne had the fellowship of the church community, especially the pastor's wife and a girl friend, to encourage his active attendance. He also was assured that his prayers got higher than the ceiling!

The second touch of the Master came to Wayne in 1936 when he entered Mars Hill College in North Carolina. He was three years older than most of the students. His previous experience as a page in the US Senate and a worker in the cotton mills served him well. He found mental and spiritual discipline in college and at church. Wayne tells how his church pastor in Mars Hill Baptist Church taught him the central message of the

---

6 Wayne E. Oates, *The Struggle To Be Free*, pp. 37-38.

New Testament and how he undertook serious study in the Bible at Mars Hill College. One day in his dormitory room he read many references to God as Father in the teaching of Jesus.

Then he says, 'It dawned upon me that in the Word become flesh in Jesus I had full membership in the family of God who is my Father in the realm of heaven, which is a revealed dimension of life here and now and forever. I ceased to be loaded down by the burden of being fatherless ... This was the time of my real conversion.'[7]

Wayne graduated from Mars Hill College in 1938 and became a student at Wake Forest College. His study courses included Greek and Latin, English literature, marriage and family, psychology and philosophy. During his college studies he learned, 'I could never be a yea-sayer, a pack thinker, a pawn of propaganda, a worshiper of ... the idols of the marketplace. Prayer became to me that internal action in which I sought to discern the intentions of God amid the hidden and manifest persuaders with smooth rhetoric.'[8]

By the time he graduated from Wake Forest College in 1940, he was ready to teach there during the week and serve two country churches full-time in summer and part-time in winter. Ahead of him lay doctoral studies and a distinguished career of teaching at the Southern Baptist Theological Seminary for thirty-five years and at the University of Louisville for eighteen years.

---

[7] Ibid., pp. 42-43.

[8] Ibid., p. 53.

Reflection

Think about the physical challenges of human blindness.

Prayer

Lord, if we are like the blind man who needed a second touch of the Master to see fully, give us sight and insight. Amen.

11   An Epileptic Boy

When they came to the disciples, they saw a great crowd around them, and some scribes arguing with them. When the whole crowd saw him, they were immediately overcome with awe, and they ran forward to greet him. He asked them, 'What are you arguing about with them?' Someone from the crowd answered him, 'Teacher, I brought you my son; he has a spirit that makes him unable to speak; and whenever it seizes him, it dashes him down; and he foams and grinds his teeth and becomes rigid; and I asked your disciples to cast it out, but they could not do so.' He answered them, 'You faithless generation, how much longer must I be among you? How much longer must I put up with you? Bring him to me.' And they brought the boy to him. When the spirit saw him, immediately it convulsed the boy, and he fell on the ground and rolled about, foaming at the mouth. Jesus asked the father, 'How long has this been happening to him?' And he said, 'From childhood. It has often cast him into the fire and into the water, to destroy him; but if you are able to do anything, have pity on us and help us.' Jesus said to him, 'If you are able!—All things can be done for the one who believes.' Immediately the father of the child cried out, 'I believe; help my unbelief!' When Jesus saw that a crowd came running together, he rebuked the unclean spirit, saying to it, 'You spirit that keeps this boy from speaking and hearing, I command you, come out of him, and never enter him again!' After crying out and convulsing him terribly, it came out, and the boy was like a corpse, so that most of them said, 'He is dead.' But Jesus took him by the hand and lifted him up, and he was able to stand. When he had entered the house, his disciples asked him privately, 'Why could we not cast it out?' He said to them, 'This kind can come out only through prayer.'
(Mark 9:14-29; compare Matthew 17:14-21; Luke 9:37-43a; Aland, *Synopsis* # 163)

Telling the Story

As Alan Culpepper indicates, the story is told in four stages.[1] First, Jesus comes down from the Mount of the Transfiguration (Mark 9:2-10) with the three disciples, Peter, James and John. After discussing matters arising from the experience, they meet the other nine disciples who are involved in an argument with

---

[1] R. Alan Culpepper, *Mark*, p. 302.

some experts in the Mosaic law. Jesus asks, *'What are you arguing about with them?'*

Second, Jesus is told by a member of the crowd, *'Teacher, I brought you my son; he has a spirit that makes him unable to speak; and whenever it seizes him, it dashes him down; and he foams and grinds his teeth and becomes rigid; and I asked your disciples to cast it out, but they could not do so.'* Jesus, annoyed at the inability of the disciples to deal with the issue, says, *'You faithless generation, how much longer must I be among you? How much longer must I put up with you? Bring him to me.'* The boy suffers convulsions, falls on the ground, rolling about and foaming at the mouth, all due to an unclean spirit. Jesus asks, *'How long has this been happening to him?'* His father answers, *'From childhood ... but if you are able to do anything, have pity on us and help us.'* Jesus picks up the words *'If you are able!'* and then assures him, *'All things can be done for the one who believes.'* At once the father cries out, *'I believe; help my unbelief!'*

Third, Jesus rebukes the unclean spirit saying, *'You spirit that keeps this boy from speaking and hearing, I command you, come out of him, and never enter him again!'* After cries and convulsions the unclean spirit comes out, and the boy is left for dead. But Jesus taking him by the hand raises him up and the boy arises.

Fourth, when Jesus goes indoors his disciples ask him privately, *'Why could we not cast it out?'* Jesus replies, *'This kind can come out only through prayer.'*

Interpreting the Story

Mark has described the cause of the boy's ailment as follows: *a spirit that makes him unable to speak* and *the unclean spirit ... that keeps this boy from speaking and hearing*. Matthew calls the boy *an epileptic* who is possessed by a demon. The dual description is explained by the observation that 'in the ancient world epileptic seizure was associated with transcendent powers of the moon.'[2] Frank Stagg rightly says, 'When one is said to be possessed by a demon, as in the case of this epileptic boy, what is stressed is ... one's being overpowered or victimized by destructive forces or factors, resulting in physical and psychological (mental and emotional) disturbances.'[3]

Whereas Mark includes the criticism that the contemporary generation is *faithless*, Matthew and Luke add the word *perverse*. The attentive reader will think of Deuteronomy 32:4-6, *A faithful God, without deceit, just and upright is he; yet his degenerate children have dealt falsely with him, a perverse and crooked generation. Do you thus repay the LORD, O foolish and senseless people?* Furthermore, Mark's concluding reference to *prayer* is replaced in Matthew by a contrast between little faith and mustard seed faith. *'For truly I tell you, if you have faith the size of a mustard seed, you will say to this mountain, 'Move from here to there,' and it will move; and nothing will be impossible for you.'* Matthew is focusing on the disciples' faith, not *little faith* but *faith the size of a mustard seed*. They are not to lack confidence in God but

---

[2] Bauer et al., A *Greek-English Lexicon of the New Testament*, p. 919.

[3] Frank Stagg, 'Matthew', *The Broadman Bible Commentary*, 8:179.

to see God's kingdom in terms of 'small beginnings and great endings.'[4]

Luke's version of the story abbreviates the Markan original. At the beginning he moves directly from the transfiguration to the healing of the boy with the unclean spirit. Thereby Luke contrasts 'the chosen three blinded by the light, the remaining nine baffled by the powers of darkness'.[5] As the story progresses, in Mark and Matthew the father calls the boy *'my son'*, but in Luke he calls him *'my only son'*. At the conclusion Luke reports, *And all were astounded at the greatness of God.* The word translated *greatness* occurs only three times in the New Testament.[6] In Acts 19:27 it is used by the Ephesian silversmith, Demetrius, of the *majesty* of the goddess Artemis (Diana). In 2 Peter 1:16 it is used of the *majesty* of Christ at the transfiguration. In Luke 9:43 it is used of the *impressiveness* of the healing of the epileptic.

Experiencing the Story

When we join the epileptic's father in saying, *'I believe; help my unbelief!'* what can we do? We may turn to the experience of Glenn Hinson for guidance. In his autobiography *A Miracle of Grace* he tells of a time of severe crisis in his life as he faced the demands of doing graduate studies and teaching undergraduates in the midst of a major seminary in crisis.

---

[4] See the treatment of the parable of the mustard seed in Doug Rowston, *Things that Jesus said*, pp. 27-31.

[5] G.B. Caird, *Saint Luke,* p. 135, quoting Plummer.

[6] Bauer et al., A *Greek-English Lexicon of the New Testament*, p. 622.

The occasion was a conflict between the administration and the faculty of the Southern Baptist Theological Seminary in the late 1950s. Glenn was affected physically and vocationally. He suffered a loss of hearing at first and then a loss of voice. He also switched from teaching New Testament, including Greek, to Church History majoring in Patristics, as the seminary faculty underwent a massive changeover in the early 1960s.

A couple of Hinson's reflections on this time of immense struggle are worth quoting. 'My most significant lesson from this time of crisis was the need to let down like a swimmer to discover a buoyancy that will hold you up. The saints through the centuries remind us that we live in a sea of love, and if we trust ourselves to that like swimmers letting down into the water, we will find 'everlasting arms' and 'a mighty right hand' to hold us up.'[7]

A few pages on in Hinson's autobiography, this biblical scholar, church historian, and spiritual guide muses about his deafness and voice problems in this way: 'I believe my struggles may have tossed into the hopper the key ingredient in my teaching philosophy, to which students have responded so positively throughout my career: the conviction that we teach *students*, not *subjects*. We use our subjects to teach persons, to be sure, but the focus should always be *persons*.'[8]

Along with many other people, I am glad that Glenn Hinson passed these lessons on to his students in biblical studies,

---

[7] E. Glenn Hinson, *A Miracle of Grace*, p. 130.

[8] Ibid., pp. 134-135.

church history and contemplative spirituality. As celebrated author Frederick Buechner said, 'In the last analysis, I have always believed, it is not so much their subjects that great teachers teach as it is themselves.'[9] That was certainly true of Glenn Hinson in my experience as a doctoral student many years ago and as an avid reader of his books and articles down through the years since then.

Reflection

Think about the times of crisis we have known within our home, work, church or society.

Prayer

Lord, sometimes all that we can say is, 'We believe; help our unbelief!' At such times let us experience that you are our refuge and that underneath are your everlasting arms. Amen.

---

[9] Frederick Buechner, *Now and Then*, p. 12.

*'The Son of Man came not to be served but to serve,
and to give his life a ransom for many.'*
Mark 10:45

12 Blind Bartimaeus

They came to Jericho. As he and his disciples and a large crowd were leaving Jericho, Bartimaeus son of Timaeus, a blind beggar, was sitting by the roadside. When he heard that it was Jesus of Nazareth, he began to shout out and say, 'Jesus, Son of David, have mercy on me!' Many sternly ordered him to be quiet, but he cried out even more loudly, 'Son of David, have mercy on me!' Jesus stood still and said, 'Call him here.' And they called the blind man, saying to him, 'Take heart; get up, he is calling you.' So throwing off his cloak, he sprang up and came to Jesus. Then Jesus said to him, 'What do you want me to do for you?' The blind man said to him, 'My teacher, let me see again.' Jesus said to him, 'Go; your faith has made you well.' Immediately he regained his sight and followed him on the way.
(Mark 10:46-52; compare Matthew 20:29-34; Luke 18:35-43; Aland, *Synopsis* # 264)

Telling the Story

Jesus and his disciples come to Jericho.[1] The town is at the lowest point in the world at 250 metres (850 feet) below sea level. From Jericho Jesus and his friends faced a winding road about 28 kilometres (17 miles) long up to Jerusalem 830 metres (2500 feet) above sea level. The ruins of ancient Jericho, the oldest city in the world dating about 7000 BC, and the ruins of Jericho rebuilt in the New Testament era, exist outside today's town.

As the company leaves Jericho, a blind beggar is sitting by the wayside. Named *Bartimaeus*, Aramaic for *son of Timaeus*, he hears that *Jesus of Nazareth* is passing by and begins to cry out, *'Jesus, Son of David, have mercy on me!'* Although he is told to be silent, he cries out all the more,*'Son of David, have mercy on

---

[1] See the map of New Testament Jericho in R. Alan Culpepper, *Mark*, p. 351 and the historical and archaeological survey in Ely Levine, 'Jericho', *The New Interpreter's Dictionary of the Bible*, 3:236-240.

me!' The blind beggar is prepared to address the visitor personally once as *'Jesus'* and twice messianically as *'Son of David'*! Jesus stops and says, *'Call him here.'* The crowd responding to the request, says to Bartimaeus, *'Take heart; get up, he is calling you.'* The blind man throws off his cloak, springs up and comes to Jesus, who says, *'What do you want me to do for you?'* Bartimaeus replies, *'My teacher* [literally *My Rabbi*], *let me see again.'* Jesus responds, *'Go; your faith has made you well.'* Immediately[2] he sees again and follows him on the way.

As Mark presents the story of Bartimaeus, he is depicted as truly an admirable character and as an exemplary disciple. He speaks to Jesus by name, acknowledges him as Messiah, is willing to learn from him, displays faith, and follows him on the way to Jerusalem. Alan Culpepper notes the significance of the reference in Mark's Gospel to *the way*, 'as a metaphor for the way of discipleship, or the way to the cross.'[3]

Interpreting the Story

According to Matthew, as Jesus leaves Jericho and heads towards Jerusalem he encounters two blind men sitting by the roadside. Twice they call him *'Son of David'* and thrice they address him as *'Lord'*. Perhaps Matthew again tells of the healing of two blind men[4] in Matthew 20:29-34, in accord with

---

[2] See p. 50 n. 5.

[3] R. Alan Culpepper, *Mark*, p. 355.

[4] Matthew also tells of the healing of two demoniacs (8:28-34) and two other blind men (9:27-31).

an Old Testament dictum: *Only on the evidence of two or three witnesses shall a charge be sustained. (Deuteronomy 19:15)*

Dale Allison in his commentary on Matthew notes the ironies of Matthew's extended narrative.[5] In the previous paragraph, James and John are 'two privileged insiders' who make a request through their mother, *'Declare that these two sons of mine will sit, one at your right hand and one at your left, in your kingdom.' (Matthew 20:21)* In the central paragraph, the blind men are 'two outsiders' who make their respectful request that the crowd seeks to silence. In the next paragraph which deals with Jesus' entry into Jerusalem, the crowd which rebuked the two blind men who called out to Jesus as the Son of David, now greets Jesus with the words, *'Hosanna to the Son of David!' (Matthew 21:9)* The reader is being alerted to the crowd's fickleness.

Luke's account of the healing of the blind man locates the event on the way into Jericho. This is before Jesus passes through the town to meet Zacchaeus, a chief tax collector. Luke does not name the blind man and refines references to the accompanying disciples and crowd. He focuses on the exchange of conversation. The blind man is told, *'Jesus of Nazareth is passing by.'* He shouts, *'Jesus, Son of David, have mercy on me!'* He cries out all the more, *'Son of David, have mercy on me!'* Jesus asks, *'What do you want me to do for you?'* The blind man replies, *'Lord, let me see again.'* Jesus says, *'Receive your sight; your faith has saved you.'* The blind man sees again, follows Jesus and glorifies God. All the people join in praising God.

---

[5] Dale C. Allison, *Matthew A Shorter Commentary,* pp. 341-342.

One is reminded of the programme of the ministry enunciated in the Nazareth synagogue by Jesus: *'The Spirit of the Lord is upon me, because he has anointed me to bring good news to the poor. He has sent me to proclaim release to the captives and **recovery of sight to the blind**, to let the oppressed go free, to proclaim the year of the Lord's favour.' (Luke 4:18-19)*

Experiencing the Story

*Amazing grace! How sweet the sound
that saved a wretch like me!
I once was lost, but now am found,
was blind but now I see.*[6]

This is one of the most well known sacred songs. It was written by a man who had a wretched early life. John Newton was born in London in 1725 and at the age of seven experienced the death of his mother. When he was eleven he went to sea with his father. By the age of nineteen he joined the Royal Navy but shortly after he deserted, was discharged, took up service with a slave trader, and in his early twenties became captain of a ship transporting slaves to America from Africa.

In 1748 his ship was caught in a severe storm. As the ship was in danger of sinking, Newton cried out to God for mercy. The captain and crew survived. Newton continued to serve on slave ships with the forlorn hope of restraining the cruel treatment of African slaves.

---

[6] See Max Cryer, *Love Me Tender: The stories behind the world's favourite songs*, pp. 68-72.

In 1755 he left his job at sea and worked in a Liverpool office. Influenced by John and Charles Wesley, and with his faith deepened, his disgust with the slave trade hardened. He now prepared himself for the Christian ministry. In 1764 he became curate of the Olney parish in Buckinghamshire. William Cowper and John Newton formed a hymn writing partnership which resulted in a popular hymnbook.

One of the hymns was entitled, 'Faith's Review and Expectation' and it was in time renamed 'Amazing Grace'. It is thought to reflect Newton's rescue from the storm at sea and his eventual renunciation of the horrors of the slave trade. In 1787 he published *Thoughts upon the African Slave Trade* in support of William Wilberforce's campaign against it. John Newton died in 1807. Ironically, he had become blind in old age. However, he knew the reality of God's amazing grace, as did the blind man who gained his sight again outside Jericho.

Reflection

Think about the ways in which we address each other formally and personally.

Prayer

Lord, help us to speak to you by name, to acknowledge you as God's Messiah, to be willing to learn from you, and to put our faith into practice as we follow you. Amen.

Part 3: Miracles in Luke's Gospel

A Prayer for Readers of Luke's Gospel[1]

Living God of Luke's Good News about Jesus, we thank you for Jesus, the burden bearer and the universal friend. Anoint us with your Spirit to receive and to share with the needy your good news. Let us experience your transforming power to carry burdens and to be friends in the name of Jesus. Amen.

---

[1] Doug Rowston, *A Bird's Eye View of the Bible Second Edition*, p. 147.

13 A Catch of Fish

Once while Jesus was standing beside the lake of Gennesaret, and the crowd was pressing in on him to hear the word of God, he saw two boats there at the shore of the lake; the fishermen had gone out of them and were washing their nets. He got into one of the boats, the one belonging to Simon, and asked him to put out a little way from the shore. Then he sat down and taught the crowds from the boat. When he had finished speaking, he said to Simon, 'Put out into the deep water and let down your nets for a catch.' Simon answered, 'Master, we have worked all night long but have caught nothing. Yet if you say so, I will let down the nets.' When they had done this, they caught so many fish that their nets were beginning to break. So they signalled their partners in the other boat to come and help them. And they came and filled both boats, so that they began to sink. But when Simon Peter saw it, he fell down at Jesus' knees, saying, 'Go away from me, Lord, for I am a sinful man!' For he and all who were with him were amazed at the catch of fish that they had taken; and so also were James and John, sons of Zebedee, who were partners with Simon. Then Jesus said to Simon, 'Do not be afraid; from now on you will be catching people.' When they had brought their boats to shore, they left everything and followed him. (Luke 5:1-11; Aland, *Synopsis* # 41)

Telling the Story

The story begins with Jesus teaching a crowd by Lake Galilee. Luke in Greek calls it *the lake of Gennesaret* reflecting the Hebrew *the sea of Chinnereth* as in Numbers 34:11 and Joshua 13:27. Here the crowd presses in on Jesus *to hear the word of God* and he embarks on Simon's boat making it a pulpit from which to teach the people on the shore.

The story continues with its focus on Simon and his partners in the fishing trade. After concluding his speech to the crowd, Jesus instructs Simon, *'Put out into the deep water and let down your nets for a catch.'* Simon is not easily persuaded and answers, *'Master, we have worked all night long but have caught nothing. Yet if you say so, I will let down the nets.'*

'Put out into the deep water and let down your nets for a catch.'

However, much to his surprise when he complies Simon and his team catch so many fish that their nets begin to break. They motion to their partners in another boat to assist them. Both boats are filled with fish and are in danger of sinking.

The story concludes with a challenging invitation to Simon, James and John. Simon is given his full name *Simon Peter*. Is this because the connection between his call to discipleship and his renaming by Jesus as Peter is being recognised? After the catch he falls down in front of Jesus and says, *'Go away from me, Lord, for I am a sinful man!'* Simon and his team as well as his fishing partners James and John are astonished at the catch. Jesus then issues his challenge to Simon, *'Do not be afraid; from now on you will be catching people.'* When all is in order with the boats on shore and the nets packed, Simon, James and John leave everything to follow Jesus.

Interpreting the Story

Looking back we find interesting Old Testament parallels. As Joel Green notes, there is a similarity between Luke 5 and Isaiah 6.[1] The miracle causes Peter to recognise Jesus as Lord and himself as sinful. The encouraging and commissioning saying of Jesus leads to Peter, James and John becoming followers of Jesus.

Christians believe that the encounter of God in Christ with our world has the same three features which the encounter of God had with the prophets. First, God was revealed in his majesty. Second, God stooped down to people. Third, God sent forth his messengers. Simon Peter is one with the school of the prophets as he encounters Jesus by the lake.

---

[1] Joel B. Green, *The Gospel of Luke*, p. 233.

Luke 5:1-11		Isaiah 6:1-10
When he had finished speaking, he said to Simon, 'Put out into the deep water and let down your nets for a catch.' Simon answered, 'Master, we have worked all night long but have caught nothing. Yet if you say so, I will let down the nets.' When they had done this, they caught so many fish that their nets were beginning to break.	Epiphany	*In the year that King Uzziah died, I saw the Lord sitting on a throne, high and lofty; and the hem of his robe filled the temple. Seraphs were in attendance above him. And one called to another and said:'Holy, holy, holy is the LORD of hosts; the whole earth is full of his glory.'*
Simon Peter fell down at Jesus' knees, saying, 'Go away from me, Lord, for I am a sinful man!'	Reaction	*I said: 'Woe is me! I am lost, for I am a man of unclean lips, yet my eyes have seen the King, the LORD of hosts!'*
Then Jesus said to Simon, 'Do not be afraid.'	Reassurance	*The seraph touched my mouth with it and said: 'Now that this has touched your lips, your guilt has departed and your sin is blotted out.'*
Jesus also said to Simon, 'From now on you will be catching people.'	Commission	*Then I heard the voice of the Lord saying, 'Whom shall I send, and who will go for us?' And I said, 'Here am I; send me!' And he said, 'Go.'*

Another Old Testament parallel is in the reference to catching people. For example, *I am now sending for many fishermen, says the LORD, and they shall catch them. (Jeremiah 16:16)* But, as Joel Green remarks, 'Disciples will no longer catch dead fish in order to sell them in the market-place, but will catch people, giving them liberty.[2]

Looking sideways we see intriguing New Testament parallels. The accounts in Matthew 4:18-22 and Mark 1:16-20 tell of the call of Simon and Andrew, James and John by the lakeside to become followers of Jesus, but there is no mention of a miraculous catch of fish. Matthew and Mark emphasise the response of these two sets of brothers each as an act of radical obedience. In the words of Howard Marshall, 'Luke's story shows that the call took place only after the fishermen had made the acquaintance of Jesus and experienced a revelation of his heavenly power.'[3]

Then there is a similar account in John 21:1-11. It has a miraculous catch of 153 fish and an implied message about the missionary task of followers of Jesus. Some scholars interpret the event as a post-resurrection happening which Luke has inserted into the record of the ministry of Jesus.[4] Other scholars interpret the Johannine account as a post-resurrection event and the Lukan account as an event in the ministry of Jesus. For example, Howard Marshall cites a study by the pre-eminent Welsh scholar, C.H. Dodd, that Luke's version 'lacks

---

[2] Ibid., p. 235.

[3] I. Howard Marshall, *The Gospel of Luke*, p. 199.

[4] R. Alan Culpepper, 'The Gospel of Luke', *The New Interpreter's Bible*, 9:116-117. Compare Raymond E. Brown, *The Gospel of John*, 2:1089-1090.

the essential "form" of a resurrection story and must be placed in the pre-resurrection period.'5

One must admit that the relationship between the passages in Matthew 4, Mark 1, Luke 5, and John 21 is complicated but the overall meaning is clear. Jesus is the one powerful in both word and deed. He draws men and women to himself and to the work of his kingdom before and after his resurrection.

Experiencing the Story

In 1999 the word 'Eternity' was prominently displayed on the Sydney Harbour Bridge as part of the New Year's Eve fireworks and again at the opening ceremony of the Sydney Olympics in September 2000 in Stadium Australia. Spectators who were present and countless millions who watched on television became aware of the legacy of a truly unique Sydneysider, Arthur Stace, 'Mr Eternity'. He was an example of someone drawn to Jesus and to the work of his kingdom. His story has been told in a remarkable book by Roy Williams with Elizabeth Meyers. As I mention a few details, I encourage my readers to obtain a copy for themselves.6

Arthur Stace was born in 1885 into a dysfunctional family. He was given up to foster care at the age of seven and had a chequered childhood. By the time he was eighteen 'no

---

5 I. Howard Marshall, *The Gospel of Luke*, p. 200.

6 Roy Williams with Elizabeth Meyers, *Mr Eternity The Story of Arthur Stace*.

employer would keep him, so he moved from job to job, from town to town - always finding a new job - a new hotel - a new policeman - and a new jail!'[7] At this stage Arthur returned to Sydney and his life continued in a downward spiral. His problems with alcohol intensified and his associations with the Sydney underworld strengthened. His dissolute father died in 1908 and his degenerate mother died in 1912. Arthur enlisted in the Australian Infantry Forces in 1916. It gave him something to do other than break the law! In early 1917 Arthur probably served as a stretcher bearer on the Western Front in France before he contracted pleurisy and was transferred to hospitals in England. After leaving hospital, he did administrative chores in London and then was repatriated after the armistice. Back in Sydney, Arthur continued in his wayward ways through the 1920s. But there was light at the end of the tunnel.

On August 6, 1930 Arthur was attracted to an evening meeting for needy men by the promise of a cup of tea and a rock cake at St Barnabas' Church on Broadway in Sydney. Rev. R. B. S. Hammond, the Rector of St Barnabas', was the speaker to the three hundred men that night who waited in turn for their cuppa and cake. Apparently Hammond captured his audience's attention in a simple and direct presentation of the good news that God loves us and provides the way of salvation through Jesus' death. Hammond concluded with an invitation, 'If any of you men are sick of the lives you are living, there is One who

---

[7] Ibid., p. 36.

loves you who will set you free and His name is Jesus.'[8] After having his cuppa and cake, Arthur walked across the street, went into Victoria Park, knelt under a large fig tree in the dark, and tearfully prayed, 'God, God be merciful to me a sinner!'[9] A day or so later, Arthur went back to St Barnabas' and made himself known to Hammond. Arthur engaged in personal prayer and Bible reading and lived obediently dispensing with his former vices. As Arthur worked with Hammond, he became a truly transformed character.

On November 14, 1932 Arthur attended the second night of an evangelistic campaign at the Burton Street Baptist Tabernacle in Darlinghurst. The speaker was Evangelist John Gotch Ridley, a recipient of the Military Cross for deeds of valour on the Western Front in 1918. The gathering of about four hundred listened to Ridley's sermon entitled 'Echoes of Eternity'. Ridley based his message on the one occurrence of the word 'eternity' in the King James Bible: *For thus saith the high and lofty One that inhabiteth eternity, whose name is Holy; I dwell in the high and holy place, with him also that is of a contrite and humble spirit, to revive the spirit of the humble, and to revive the heart of the contrite ones. (Isaiah 57:15)*[10] Ridley spoke of the echoes of eternity in creation, the Christian, and the cross. He

---

[8] Ibid., p. 99.

[9] Ibid., p. 100.

[10] The word occurs in the New Revised Standard Version of the Bible three times: Isaiah 45:17; 57:15; 2 Peter 3:18. It also occurs six times in the NRSV Apocrypha.

concluded with the plea, 'Eternity! Eternity! I wish that I could sound, or shout, that word to everyone on the streets of Sydney. Eternity! Friends, you have got to meet it. Where will you spend Eternity?'[11] After Arthur Stace left the meeting he wrote the word 'Eternity' with a piece of chalk on the footpath outside the church. So began Arthur's habit of rising early, praying, eating breakfast, going to a selected area of Sydney and writing the word on its footpaths for a period of two or more hours.

The rest of Arthur's story is well told by Williams and Meyers. There are such things as his writing 'Eternity' in chalk on footpaths and other public places, his involvement in the work of St Barnabas', his transition to the Burton Street Tabernacle, his marriage to Pearl, his preaching in both the open air and in churches, his work with Lisle Thompson who was pastor of Burton Street, the death of Pearl after eighteen years of marriage, and his move to a nursing home. Arthur Stace in his own way experienced a miraculous change in his life and sought to follow Jesus as a messenger of the good news by means of the word 'Eternity'. As Bernard Judd wrote on the morning of Arthur's funeral in 1967, 'The last 37 years of his life were an outstanding example of the saving and keeping power of Jesus Christ.'[12]

---

[11] Roy Williams with Elizabeth Meyers, *Mr Eternity The Story of Arthur Stace*, p. 112.

[12] Ibid., p. 208.

Reflection

Think about the ideas of God's majesty, God stooping down to people, and God sending forth his messengers.

Prayer

Lord, help us to experience the realities of your glory, your coming in Jesus, and your sending us out with your message. Amen.

14   A Widow's Son

Soon afterwards he went to a town called Nain, and his disciples and a large crowd went with him. As he approached the gate of the town, a man who had died was being carried out. He was his mother's only son, and she was a widow; and with her was a large crowd from the town. When the Lord saw her, he had compassion for her and said to her, 'Do not weep.' Then he came forward and touched the bier, and the bearers stood still. And he said, 'Young man, I say to you, rise!' The dead man sat up and began to speak, and Jesus gave him to his mother. Fear seized all of them; and they glorified God, saying, 'A great prophet has risen among us!' and 'God has looked favourably on his people!' This word about him spread throughout Judea and all the surrounding country.
(Luke 7:11-17; Aland, *Synopsis* # 86)

Telling the Story

First, there is a tragic situation. The location is *Nain* about ten kilometres (six miles) south-east of Nazareth. At the gate of Nain a dead man is being carried out on a stretcher to his burial. The dead man is *his mother's only son*, and even worse, she is *a widow*. A large crowd from Nain is accompanying her. She is in dire straits as she has lost her husband and her only son. She has every reason to weep and wail for she has lost her place in the town community, now having no visible means of support. One thinks of the need for first century Christians to heed the injunction: *Religion that is pure and undefiled before God, the Father, is this: to care for orphans and widows in their distress, and to keep oneself unstained by the world. (James 1:27)*

Second, there is the intervention of Jesus. When Jesus, who is called *Lord* by Luke, sees the widow he has *compassion* for her and says, *'Do not weep.'* Throughout Luke's Gospel Jesus is identified as *Lord*. 'The use of the term reflects the designation of Jesus in the early church as the one exalted by God to be the Lord ... and indicates that already during his earthly ministry Jesus was exercising the functions of the Lord.'[1] Accordingly Jesus acts with compassionate power. He touches the stretcher on which the corpse is being carried and the bearers stand still. Jesus speaks, *'Young man, I say to you, rise!'* The dead man sits up and speaks and then Jesus gives him back to his mother.

Finally, there is the distinctive response of the onlookers; fear seizes the entire crowd and they give glory to God by saying, *'A great prophet has risen among us!'* and *'God has looked favourably on his people!'* Luke concludes this miracle story with reference to reports going *throughout Judea and all the surrounding country.* In Luke 1:5; 4:44: 7:17; 23:5, the Gospel writer refers to 'Judea, broadly understood as the region occupied by the people of Israel, Judea = "land of the Judeans (Jews)", i.e. Palestine.'[2]

Interpreting the Story

Once more we find interesting Old Testament parallels. In 1 Kings 17:17-24 and 2 Kings 4:18-37 similar stories are told of two prophets.

---

[1] I. Howard Marshall, *The Gospel of Luke*, p. 285.

[2] Bauer et al., A *Greek-English Lexicon of the New Testament*, p. 478.

First, during a drought Elijah lodges in the home of a widow of Zarephath where the household is miraculously maintained on a jar of meal and jug of oil until the breaking of the drought. However, the widow's son dies. The prophet takes the boy to the upper chamber and prays. After stretching himself on the child three times and praying to God, Elijah receives a response, the child revives. The prophet brings the boy down from the upper chamber and gives him to his mother who says, *'Now I know that you are a man of God, and that the word of the LORD in your mouth is truth.'(1 Kings 17:24)*

Second, Elisha during his travels often stays in the home of a Shunammite woman and her old husband with a small roof chamber provided for him. The woman is childless and the prophet promises that in due time she shall have a son and the promise is fulfilled. The years pass and on a certain day the boy in going to the field with his father suffers a headache and dies. Once the boy is brought home and is laid on the prophet's bed in the upper chamber, the mother goes to fetch the prophet at Mount Carmel. Elisha's return is preceded by his servant who tries unsuccessfully to revive the boy. Elisha comes, prays, performs mouth to mouth resuscitation, and the boy becomes warm, sneezes seven times, opens his eyes, and is restored to his mother.

As George Caird says succinctly, 'Jesus was a great prophet because he had done what Elijah and Elisha did.'[3] Luke's

---

[3] G.B. Caird, *Saint Luke,* p. 109.

narrative continues with a visit of two disciples of John the Baptist who are sent to ask Jesus if he is the one who is to come. Jesus replies, *'Go and tell John what you have seen and heard: the blind receive their sight, the lame walk, the lepers are cleansed, the deaf hear, the dead are raised, the poor have good news brought to them.' (Luke 7:22)* Alan Culpepper by means of a table shows that throughout Luke's Gospel are echoes of the Elijah and Elisha stories and passages in the book of Isaiah, the latter especially from chapters 29, 35, and 61.[4] Indeed, it may be said that the Old Testament promises what the New Testament fulfils. In the ministry of Jesus, the messianic age has dawned and God's kingdom is coming.

Experiencing the Story

In his reflections on Jesus' statement, *'Young man, I say to you, rise!'* Culpepper notes the echoes of this statement in New Testament references to the raising of Jesus such as Acts 2:32 and 1 Corinthians 15:20. As Culpepper says, 'The hope of the resurrection ... is not grounded in the fact that the widow's son came back to life but in the fact that the one who had the compassion to bring back the widow's son has himself triumphed over death.'[5]

---

[4] R. Alan Culpepper, 'The Gospel of Luke', *The New Interpreter's Bible*, 9:161.

[5] Ibid., p.159.

The rediscovery of the centrality of the resurrection in twentieth century Christian thought was largely due to the groundbreaking work of Jürgen Moltmann in his book, *Theologie die Hoffnung*. It was originally published in German in 1964 and the English translation *Theology of Hope* followed in 1967. As Moltmann says in his autobiography, 'I believe that three concepts are essential for every Christian theology of hope: 1. the concept of *the divine promise*, 2. the concept of *the raising of the crucified Christ* as God's promise for the world, 3. an understanding of human history as *the mission of the kingdom of God*.'[6] Moltmann's next two books, *The Crucified God*[7] and *The Church in the Power of the Spirit*[8], were also warmly welcomed by the Academy and the Church. Since then Jürgen Moltmann has continued to write prolifically and to contribute to the life of the worldwide Christian community.

Moltmann experienced for himself the truth of the story of a widow's son. He endured a 1943 firestorm in Hamburg, he experienced the horror of war as a young German conscript, he found faith in a Scottish Prisoner of War camp, he became a theological student and then a church pastor in Germany. Following his marriage to Elisabeth, they suffered the death of their first child at birth, and were fortunate to have three other children as he made the transition from the pastorate to

---

[6] Jürgen Moltmann, *A Broad Place*, p.101.

[7] German original 1972, English translation 1974.

[8] German original 1975, English translation 1977.

seminary life as a professor. In other words, Jürgen Moltmann has lived a full life.

Reflection

From the beginning to the ending of our lives, think about the challenges that we face.

Prayer

Lord, help young and old to find their hope in your promises as set forth in the life, death, and resurrection of Jesus. Amen.

15   A Crippled Woman

Now he was teaching in one of the synagogues on the sabbath. And just then there appeared a woman with a spirit that had crippled her for eighteen years. She was bent over and was quite unable to stand up straight. When Jesus saw her, he called her over and said, 'Woman, you are set free from your ailment.' When he laid his hands on her, immediately she stood up straight and began praising God. But the leader of the synagogue, indignant because Jesus had cured on the sabbath, kept saying to the crowd, 'There are six days on which work ought to be done; come on those days and be cured, and not on the sabbath day.' But the Lord answered him and said, 'You hypocrites! Does not each of you on the sabbath untie his ox or his donkey from the manger, and lead it away to give it water? And ought not this woman, a daughter of Abraham whom Satan bound for eighteen long years, be set free from this bondage on the sabbath day?' When he said this, all his opponents were put to shame; and the entire crowd was rejoicing at all the wonderful things that he was doing.
(Luke 13:10-17; Aland, *Synopsis* # 208)

Telling the Story

The situation of the story is that Jesus is teaching in a synagogue, the place of worship, on the sabbath, the day of rest. The timing is reinforced by a fivefold reference to the sabbath. A woman appears on the scene who has been crippled *with a spirit* for eighteen years. By mention of *a spirit* her condition is attributed to an evil influence. She is bent over, unable to stand up straight. She could be suffering from 'a fusion of the spinal bones.'[1]

The action in the story is provided by Jesus. He sees the crippled woman, calls her to him and says, *'Woman, you are set free from your ailment.'* He lays his hands on her. She stands up

---

[1] I. Howard Marshall, *The Gospel of Luke*, p. 557.

straight and begins to praise God. In Acts, the sequel to the Gospel of Luke, Peter speaks of *'how God anointed Jesus of Nazareth with the Holy Spirit and with power; how he went about doing good and healing all who were oppressed by the devil, for God was with him.' (Acts 10:38).* The crippled woman would agree wholeheartedly.

The argument in the story occurs between the synagogue ruler and Jesus. The ruler tells the congregation that the sabbath is a day of rest, not a day of work; healing can be done on another day. Jesus reasons if animals may be cared for on the sabbath, *'ought not this woman, a daughter of Abraham whom Satan bound for eighteen long years, be set free from this bondage on the sabbath day?'* Tellingly, Jesus introduces his reasoning with the accusation, *'You hypocrites!'* Those who agree with the synagogue leader care for animals but not for *'a daughter of Abraham'.*

The ending of the story is shame to the leader of the synagogue and the opponents of Jesus and honour to Jesus and the woman. The whole crowd is rejoicing at all the marvellous things that Jesus is doing. As Alan Culpepper remarks, 'Because of her physical condition, the woman carried shame, but by the end of the story she has been released from her shame and Jesus' opponents have been shamed.'[2]

---

[2] R. Alan Culpepper, 'The Gospel of Luke', *The New Interpreter's Bible*, 9:274.

Interpreting the Story

The evangelist has introduced the ministry of Jesus with a programmatic statement: *'The Spirit of the Lord is upon me, because he has anointed me to bring good news to the poor. He has sent me to proclaim release to the captives and recovery of sight to the blind, to let the oppressed go free, to proclaim the year of the Lord's favour.'(Luke 4:18-19)*

This uniquely Lukan story of a crippled woman is a telling example of letting the oppressed go free. First, not only is there physical restoration for the woman but there is honourable recognition for her in society. After eighteen years she is physically no longer bent over for she is now able to stand up straight. Furthermore, as Jesus treats her 'with a proper sense of dignity, freedom, and worth'[3] she is now publicly called *'a daughter of Abraham'*. The crippled woman is one among many women mentioned in Luke's narrative which features women prominently. We are told that as Jesus ministers in word and deed he is accompanied by the twelve disciples *as well as some women who had been cured of evil spirits and infirmities: Mary, called Magdalene, from whom seven demons had gone out, and Joanna, the wife of Herod's steward Chuza, and Susanna, and many others, who provided for them out of their resources. (Luke 8:2-3)*

---

[3] Evelyn and Frank Stagg, *Woman in the World of Jesus*, p. 106.

Second, the matter of sabbath observance is put in perspective. As Evelyn and Frank Stagg indicate, 'Here is a basic clue to understanding Jesus. The personal, whether God or a human being, always took priority over things and over religion itself. A woman was a person, that first.'[4] Accordingly, Jesus says to her on a sabbath day, *'Woman, you are set free from your ailment.'* In Luke the keeping of a sabbath rest is critiqued by Jesus as he claims to be lord of the sabbath (Luke 6:5), and he heals on the sabbath (Luke 6:9; 13:14; 14:3). Culpepper comments, 'Sabbath observance is defined positively, not in terms of what one will not do, but in terms of what one must do.'[5] As we shall see, the same applies in two of the signs performed on a sabbath in John's Gospel (John 5:16; 9:16).

Experiencing the Story

How can one person read the Bible one way and another person read it in a diametrically opposite way? In the story of the crippled woman the synagogue ruler reads the scriptural regulations about sabbath observance negatively, that is, what should not be done. Jesus, on the other hand, reads them positively, that is, what should be done. When I reflect on this issue I am reminded of a fellow teacher and his life experiences. David Mattingley's story has been told by his wife

---

[4] Ibid., p. 107.

[5] R. Alan Culpepper, 'The Gospel of Luke', *The New Interpreter's Bible*, 9:135.

in a truly fascinating book.⁶ However, I did not learn the details of David's life until I read the book after his funeral in 2017. All I knew was the quiet and humble man who taught English and History at Prince Alfred College for thirty-two years and then lived in retirement at Stoneyfell until his death at the age of ninety-four.

In fact, David was a war hero. He flew twenty-three missions as a bomber pilot over Nazi Germany. His last flight was eventful to say the least. David was awarded the Distinguished Flying Cross. The official citation for the award reads as follows:

As pilot and captain of an aircraft, Flying Officer MATTINGLEY took part in an attack against DORTMUND in November, 1944. Whilst over the target, the aircraft was badly hit and Flying Officer MATTINGLEY was wounded about the head, arm and thigh. In spite of the hits he carried on and afterwards flew the damaged aircraft back to the United Kingdom. His indomitable spirit, superb captaincy and outstanding devotion to duty set an example of high order.⁷

David was only twenty-two years old at the time. He would spend nearly three years in hospitals in both England and Tasmania.

---

⁶ Christobel Mattingley, *Battle Order 204: A bomber pilot's story*.

⁷ Ibid., p. 244.

A couple of references in *Battle Order 204* suggest that David had learned to read the Bible positively. One reference relates that on his flights 'David carried the small black Bible he had bought at St Paul's Cathedral in Melbourne ... It fitted snugly in the left-hand pocket of his battledress, just over his heart.'[8] During his hospitalisation his brother visited him and the two of them went to Lincoln Cathedral where they sat and listened to a choir sing Handel's *Messiah*. 'David felt washed, bathed, soaked, shaped in its healing affirmation. He truly knew that his Redeemer lived and whatever might happen, held him in His almighty love.'[9]

Reflection

Think about different approaches that are taken in reading the Bible: discovering its historical context, examining its literary meaning, and investigating its interpretation down through the years.

Prayer

Lord, remind us that you speak sometimes in signs, sometimes in silence, often in the Bible, and always in Jesus. Amen.

---

[8] Ibid., p. 226.

[9] Ibid., p. 251.

16   A Swollen Man

On one occasion when Jesus was going to the house of a leader of the Pharisees to eat a meal on the sabbath, they were watching him closely. Just then, in front of him, there was a man who had dropsy. And Jesus asked the lawyers and Pharisees, 'Is it lawful to cure people on the sabbath, or not?' But they were silent. So Jesus took him and healed him, and sent him away. Then he said to them, 'If one of you has a child or an ox that has fallen into a well, will you not immediately pull it out on a sabbath day?' And they could not reply to this.
(Luke 14:1-6; Aland, *Synopsis* # 214)

Telling the Story

The setting is the home of a leading Pharisee where Jesus has been invited to dine on a sabbath. Jesus is under surveillance by the religious authorities and he encounters a man who suffers from dropsy or edema. As Joel Green explains, dropsy 'refers to bodily swelling due to an excess of fluid; not a disease itself, dropsy is an indication of malfunction in the body, especially congestive heart failure or kidney disease.'[1]

The silence of the religious authorities results from a question of Jesus, *'Is it lawful to cure people on the sabbath, or not?'* The sabbath healing of the swollen man by Jesus is clinched by his statement, *'If one of you has a child or an ox that has fallen into a well, will you not immediately pull it out on a sabbath day?'*

---

[1] Joel B. Green, *The Gospel of Luke*, p. 546.

Interpreting the Story

Luke tells three stories about healing on the sabbath. The first is of a man with a withered hand (Luke 6:6-11); and the second and third involve a crippled woman and a swollen man (Luke 13:10-17 and 14:1-6). There are similarities between the second and third stories about the woman and the man.[2]

A crippled woman (Luke 13:10-17)	A swollen man (Luke 14:1-6)
Jesus is teaching in a synagogue on the sabbath.	Jesus is dining in a home on the sabbath.
The leader of the synagogue is present.	A leader of the Pharisees is present.
Jesus asks a question, *'Ought not this woman be set free from this bondage on the sabbath?'*	Jesus asks a question, *'Is it lawful to cure people on the sabbath, or not?'*
Jesus uses an analogy about the treatment of animals on the sabbath.	Jesus uses an analogy about the treatment of a child or an animal on the sabbath.

Whether the person who encounters Jesus is male or female, whether the setting is religious or domestic, Jesus is the bearer of the Spirit of the Lord who brings good news to the poor, proclaims release to the captives and recovery of sight to the blind, lets the oppressed go free, and proclaims the time of the

---

[2] Ibid., pp. 543-544.

Lord's favour. Whenever people exercise their sight, whenever people listen attentively, the ministry of Jesus issues in the blind receiving their sight, the lame walking, the lepers being cleansed, the deaf hearing, the dead being raised, and the poor having good news brought to them. Such is the programme of Luke's version of the story of Jesus.[3]

Experiencing the Story

Whether it is teaching in a synagogue on the sabbath or dining in a home on the sabbath, Jesus has a sense of priority: people matter more than things. Unfortunately, the leader in the synagogue and a leader of the Pharisees seem to have the opposite attitude: things matter more than people.

In his autobiography Glenn Hinson draws a similar contrast between two Popes. On the one hand, he recalls the impact of Pope John XXIII through the Second Vatican Council which began in 1962. The Pope's opening address included these words: 'For with the opening of this Council a new day is dawning on the Church, bathing her in radiant splendor. It is yet the dawn, but the sun in its rising has already set our hearts aglow. All around us is the fragrance of holiness and joy.'[4] For Hinson John XXIII was indeed a leader to whom people mattered more than things.

On the other hand, Hinson retells an ironic imaginary story which was popular among American Catholics and has to do

---

[3] Compare Luke 4:18-19; 7:22.

[4] E. Glenn Hinson, *A Miracle of Grace*, p. 226.

with the unravelling of the reforms of the Second Vatican Council by the Polish Pope John Paul II. The story went as follows. God was willing to answer three of John Paul II's questions. First, the pope asked, 'Will there be married priests in my lifetime?' God answered, 'No, not in your lifetime.' Second, the pope inquired, 'Will there be ordained women in my lifetime?' God replied, 'No, not in your lifetime.' Finally, the pope said, 'What I really want to know is whether there will be another Polish pope.' God responded, 'No, not in my lifetime.'[5] John Paul II was probably a leader to whom certain things mattered more than people.

Reflection

Think about priorities that we set in terms of people and things.

Prayer

Lord, guide us as we sort out the important and the unimportant in our dealings with people and things. Amen.

---

[5] Ibid., pp. 274-275.

17 Ten Lepers

On the way to Jerusalem Jesus was going through the region between Samaria and Galilee. As he entered a village, ten lepers approached him. Keeping their distance, they called out, saying, 'Jesus, Master, have mercy on us!' When he saw them, he said to them, 'Go and show yourselves to the priests.' And as they went, they were made clean. Then one of them, when he saw that he was healed, turned back, praising God with a loud voice. He prostrated himself at Jesus' feet and thanked him. And he was a Samaritan. Then Jesus asked, 'Were not ten made clean? But the other nine, where are they? Was none of them found to return and give praise to God except this foreigner?' Then he said to him, 'Get up and go on your way; your faith has made you well.'
(Luke 17:11-19; Aland, *Synopsis* # 233)

Telling the Story[1]

First, ten lepers approach Jesus as he goes from Galilee through Samaria on to Judea and its capital Jerusalem. In the time of Jesus the Jews consider Samaritans to be unclean and believe that contact with Samaritans renders them ritually impure. As the Fourth Gospel notes, *Jews do not share things in common with Samaritans. (John 4:9)* There is no love lost between Jews and Samaritans. There is also no love lost between healthy Jews and unhealthy lepers. Lepers are not wanted inside the towns and villages of Roman Palestine, which is in accord with the Levitical law, *The person who has the leprous disease shall wear torn clothes and let the hair of his head be dishevelled; and he shall cover his upper lip and cry out, 'Unclean, unclean.' He shall remain unclean as long as*

---

[1] See pp. 6-7 above for issues relating to the treatment and definition of leprosy.

he has the disease; he is unclean. He shall live alone; his dwelling shall be outside the camp. (Leviticus 13:45-46)

Second, the ten lepers have kept their distance but call out, *'Jesus, Master, have mercy on us!'* They address Jesus as *Master*. The title is used of Jesus six times in Luke 5:5 (Simon Peter); 8:24 (disciples); 8:45 (Peter); 9:33 (Peter); 9:49 (John); and 17:13 (lepers). Seeing them, Jesus responds, *'Go and show yourselves to the priests.'* Joel Green observes, 'As "health care consultants", priests functioned as "purity inspectors" to exclude persons or restore them to their social roles.'[2] On their way to the priests, the ten lepers are made clean.

Third, only one of the ten lepers, when he sees that he is healed, turns back. He praises God with a loud voice as he falls down at the feet of Jesus and thanks him. *And he was a Samaritan*. Then Jesus asks three questions, *'Were not ten made clean? But the other nine, where are they? Was none of them found to return and give praise to God except this foreigner?'* The point is that a foreigner has come to faith through gratitude and praise. Jesus encourages him with the words, *'Get up and go on your way; your faith has made you well.'* All of this comes to pass on the way to Jerusalem but only an outcast Samaritan sees its true meaning.

---

[2] Joel B. Green, *The Gospel of Luke,* p. 624.

Interpreting the Story

Here an Old Testament story comes to mind. In 2 Kings 5 Naaman, a commander of the army of the Aramean king, was a victorious warrior but he suffered from leprosy. A young Israelite girl captured in an Aramean raid is now a household servant. She tells Naaman's wife about the prophet in northern Israel who has power to heal Naaman of his skin complaint. On hearing this, Naaman obtains his king's permission to go with valuable gifts and a royal letter to the king of Israel. Of course the Israelite king is afraid of the consequences of his inability to heal the commander and Elisha hears of the king's dilemma and sends him a message to let him come *'that he may learn that there is a prophet in Israel.' (2 Kings 5:8)* So Naaman comes with his army to the door of Elisha's house and Elisha sends a message, *'Go, wash in the Jordan seven times, and your flesh shall be restored and you shall be clean.' (2 Kings 5:10)*

In anger Naaman goes away for he cannot believe that the prophet has not met him face to face and there and then called on the name of his God to cure him of his leprosy. Naaman contrasts the superior rivers of Syria with the inferior water courses of Israel. But his servants reproach him for being unwilling to obey the simple command, namely, *'Wash, and be clean.' (2 Kings 5:13)* So Naaman goes and immerses himself seven times in the River Jordan and as he does his flesh is restored and clean *like the flesh of a young boy (2 Kings 5:14)*. Naaman with his army then returns to Elisha, and standing before him says, *'Now I know that there is no God in all the earth except in Israel.'(2 Kings 5:15)*

The ten lepers like Naaman have learned that there is another prophet in Israel. They also approach this prophet with the words, *'Jesus, Master, have mercy on us!'* They are given a simple command by this prophet, *'Go and show yourselves to the priests.'* It comes to pass that as they go to find a priest they are made clean. But only one, when he sees that he is healed, turns back. Praising God loudly and falling down in front of Jesus, he thanks him. *And he was a Samaritan.* Jesus encourages him, *'Get up and go on your way; your faith has made you well.'* In this story Luke reinforces the words of Jesus to John the Baptist: *'the blind receive their sight, the lame walk, the lepers are cleansed, the deaf hear, the dead are raised, the poor have good news brought to them. And blessed is anyone who takes no offence at me.' (Luke 7:22-23)*

By reporting that the one who came back to thank Jesus was a Samaritan, Luke underlines the attitude of Jesus towards Samaritans.[3] As Joachim Jeremias says, 'We see ... that before AD 70 the Jewish attitude to the Samaritans was very much the same as their attitude to Gentiles ... Contact with Samaritans was as difficult, at least for those Jews who observed Pharisaic laws on purity, as that with Gentiles.'[4] Not only is the

---

[3] See the treatment of the parable of the Good Samaritan in Doug Rowston, *Things that Jesus said*, pp. 68-74.

[4] Joachim Jeremias, *Jerusalem in the Time of Jesus*, p. 358.

surprising hero of the famous parable in Luke 10 a Samaritan, but also the grateful cured leper in Luke 17 is a Samaritan. Jeremias sums up the contribution of Jesus tellingly. 'He put before these Jews the picture of a Samaritan as a model, humiliating for them to contemplate, of gratitude (Luke 17.17-19) and of neighbourly love triumphing over deep-rooted national hatred (Luke 10.30-37).'[5]

Experiencing the Story

Is there anybody in recent times who comes to mind as someone who cared for today's equivalents of lepers and Samaritans? By way of answer I recall the autumn of 1968 when I sat next to a man unknown to me at the time in a New Testament Departmental Colloquium at Southern Seminary in Louisville, Kentucky. His name was Clarence Jordan.[6] In due course I realised that he was truly a legend in his own short lifetime.

Jordan was born on July 29, 1912 in Talbot County, Georgia. He joined the local church at the age of twelve where he soon learned of the contradiction between the worship of white Baptists and their harsh treatment of blacks in Georgia. In 1929 he began studying agriculture at the University of Georgia in Athens. In 1933 after four years in the Reserve Officers Training Corps, he turned down the opportunity to be

---

[5] Ibid.

[6] See Joyce Hollyday, *Clarence Jordan Essential Writings*. I am indebted to this fine book for details of Jordan's life and extracts of his translations and sermons.

commissioned in the United States Cavalry. The Sermon on the Mount had convinced him to love his enemies. He went off to become a Baptist preacher studying at Southern Seminary in Louisville. He worked in inner city churches and taught at a black university. Jordan completed his Ph.D. in New Testament Greek by 1936, the same year in which he married Florence. They lived and worked in Louisville until 1942.

Then Jordan and Martin England founded Koinonia Farm, an interracial Christian community in Americus, Georgia which was a most adventurous and dangerous experiment! Despite hostility and antagonism from local neighbours, from fellow church members, and from county officials, the Koinonia community advocated pacifism and desegregation. There were threats over the phone, vandalism of communal property, verbal and physical abuse of children at school, exclusion from the local Baptist church, shootings at night, bombings of outlets, boycotts of Koinonia Farm products, and meetings of the Ku Klux Klan.

Meanwhile the Koinonia community began a mail order business to sell pecan nuts beyond the borders of Georgia. Jordan and Millard Fuller started a project to enable low income families to acquire land and build homes. In time this became 'Habitat for Humanity' with a worldwide impact. Alongside these developments, Jordan continued to read and preach, his study based on the Greek New Testament. He began to put into writing his translation of the New Testament as a 'cotton patch' version. The translation was written in terms easily understood by inhabitants of the American South who live 'in the land of cotton.'[7] When he died of a heart attack on October 29 1969, he was sitting in his writing cabin where he produced his 'cotton patch' translations. On his desk was an incomplete version of John's Gospel.

As Joyce Hollyday records, 'He was treated in death as in life - reviled by his enemies and tenderly loved by his family and friends.'[8] If ever anyone followed the example of Jesus in caring for lepers and Samaritans, it was Clarence Jordan. His 'cotton patch' version of Galatians 3:27-28 captures its meaning for his fellow southerners. 'You who were initiated into the Christian fellowship are Christian allies. No more is one a white person and another a black person; no more is one a slave and the other a free person; no longer is one a male and the other a female. For you *all* are as *one* in Christ Jesus.'[9]

In his sermons on the substance of faith Jordan paraphrases Hebrews 11:1, 'Faith is the activation of our aspirations, the life based on unseen realities. It is conviction translated into deeds. In short, it is the word become flesh.'[10] Clarence, mistakenly called a communist by so many supposed Christians, leaves a legacy which challenges racism, militarism, and materialism.

---

[7] *Dixie,* a popular song in the South, commences with the words: 'I wish I was in the land of cotton.'

[8] Joyce Hollyday, *Clarence Jordan Essential Writings.*, p. 34.

[9] Ibid., p. 90.

[10] Ibid., p. 143.

He certainly cared for today's equivalents of lepers and Samaritans in the time of Jesus.

Reflection

Think about distinctions we make between different types of people.

Prayer

Lord, teach us to treat others as people who have been made in your image and for whom Christ died on the cross and rose from the dead. Amen.

18 A Stranger on the Road

Now on that same day two of them were going to a village called Emmaus, about seven miles from Jerusalem, and talking with each other about all these things that had happened. While they were talking and discussing, Jesus himself came near and went with them, but their eyes were kept from recognising him. And he said to them, 'What are you discussing with each other while you walk along?' They stood still, looking sad. Then one of them, whose name was Cleopas, answered him, 'Are you the only stranger in Jerusalem who does not know the things that have taken place there in these days?' He asked them, 'What things?' They replied, 'The things about Jesus of Nazareth, who was a prophet mighty in deed and word before God and all the people, and how our chief priests and leaders handed him over to be condemned to death and crucified him. But we had hoped that he was the one to redeem Israel. Yes, and besides all this, it is now the third day since these things took place. Moreover, some women of our group astounded us. They were at the tomb early this morning, and when they did not find his body there, they came back and told us that they had indeed seen a vision of angels who said that he was alive. Some of those who were with us went to the tomb and found it just as the women had said; but they did not see him.' Then he said to them, 'Oh, how foolish you are, and how slow of heart to believe all that the prophets have declared! Was it not necessary that the Messiah should suffer these things and then enter into his glory?' Then beginning with Moses and all the prophets, he interpreted to them the things about himself in all the scriptures. As they came near the village to which they were going, he walked ahead as if he were going on. But they urged him strongly, saying, 'Stay with us, because it is almost evening and the day is now nearly over.' So he went in to stay with them. When he was at the table with them, he took bread, blessed and broke it, and gave it to them. Then their eyes were opened, and they recognised him; and he vanished from their sight. They said to each other, 'Were not our hearts burning within us while he was talking to us on the road, while he was opening the scriptures to us?' That same hour they got up and returned to Jerusalem; and they found the eleven and their companions gathered together. They were saying, 'The Lord has risen indeed, and he has appeared to Simon!' Then they told what had happened on the road, and how he had been made known to them in the breaking of the bread.
(Luke 24:13-35; Aland, *Synopsis* # 355)

Telling the Story

First, there is discussion between two discouraged people on the way to Emmaus. According to Luke, the village is *about seven miles* [11 kilometres] *from Jerusalem*. While they are talking and discussing the strange happenings of the day, a stranger joins them on the road. It is Jesus but they don't recognise him. He asks them, *'What are you discussing with each other while you walk along?'* They begin to converse with him, overtaken by sadness.

Second, there is conversation between the couple and the stranger which leads to instruction. Cleopas replies to the stranger, *'Are you the only stranger in Jerusalem who does not know the things that have taken place there in these days?'* When asked for clarification, the couple reply, *'The things about Jesus of Nazareth, who was a prophet mighty in deed and word before God and all the people, and how our chief priests and leaders handed him over to be condemned to death and crucified him. But we had hoped that he was the one to redeem Israel.'* The couple go on to talk about the visit of women to the tomb on this the morning of the third day, the lack of a body, the message of angels, the subsequent visit of men to the tomb, and the failure to see Jesus. The stranger then says, *'Oh, how foolish you are, and how slow of heart to believe all that the prophets have declared! Was it not necessary that the Messiah should suffer these things and then enter into his glory?'* According to Luke, the stranger gives the couple a bird's eye view of the Old Testament including a pattern of God at work with his ancient people which foreshadowed the ministry of Jesus.

Third, there is the couple's recognition of the divine presence in the stranger. As the couple approach Emmaus, the stranger walks on as if to go further. However, the couple press him to stay with them so he does. As they are all sit down, the stranger takes bread, says the blessing, breaks the bread, and offers it to them. He is a stranger no more; the couple recognise him as their Jesus and he vanishes from their sight.

Fourth, there is the couple's testimony. They say to each other, *'Were not our hearts burning within us while he was talking to us on the road, while he was opening the scriptures to us?'* With no delay the couple get up and return to Jerusalem. They join the eleven disciples who tell them of the Lord's appearance to Simon Peter. In turn the couple tell their story of the encounter with the stranger on the road and the revelation in Emmaus during the breaking of the bread.

Interpreting the Story

After the death of Jesus, but before they are aware of the reality of the resurrection of Jesus, two disciples are on their way to a village called Emmaus. The two may have been husband and wife, Cleopas and Mary, according to John 19:25. *Cleopas* [literally *Kleopas*] in Luke 24:18 is the Greek form and *Clopas* [literally *Klopas*] in John 19:25 is the Semitic form. Now we do know that the risen Jesus appears to these two going to

Emmaus. But we don't know exactly where Emmaus was. There are four possible sites.[1]

The first proposed town is **el-Qubeibeh**. It has been identified as Emmaus since 1280. It is about 7 miles/11 kilometres/ 60 stadia from Jerusalem on the road to the port of Haifa used by the Crusaders in the thirteenth century. We notice that the accepted reading in modern versions of Luke 24:13 is the equivalent of 60 stadia. A Franciscan Church was constructed in the nineteenth century on the site of an earlier church and a small castle. On Easter Monday el-Qubeibeh is the scene of a celebration by Christians of all persuasions of the appearance on the way to Emmaus. A first Emmaus can be in the experience of communal worship as people speak to the Lord in praise, giving and dedication and as the Lord speaks to people in meditation and proclamation.

The second proposed town is **Abu Ghosh**. It has been identified as Emmaus since 1141. It is also about 7 miles/11 kilometres/60 stadia from Jerusalem but it is on the road to the port of Jaffa, modern Yafo, used by the Crusaders in the twelfth century. Before their defeat at the Horns of Hattin in 1187, the Crusaders built the Church of the Resurrection at Abu Ghosh. In Old Testament times Abu Ghosh was the resting place of the Ark of the Covenant (1 Samuel 7:1-2). It was called the City of Woods, Kiriath-jearim. Today the Crusader church is the largest building in the village. The walls feature the frescoes of medieval artists. A second Emmaus can be in the beauty of a

---

[1] I am indebted to my participation in a course entitled 'The Bible and its Setting' at St George's College in August 1981 for the following details. See also Peter Walker, *In the Steps of Jesus*, pp. 204-205.

holy place as people sense the reality of the Lord in a setting with sacred associations.

The third proposed town is **Latrun** at the site of an Arab village called Imwas which was destroyed in the Six Day War of 1967. Today a picnic ground is the only reminder of the location of the village. Imwas had been identified as Emmaus since 330. It is about 20 miles/31 kilometres/160 stadia from Jerusalem and on the road to the port of Jaffa. The marginal reading of Luke 24:13, which indicates that some ancient manuscripts read 160 stadia, probably arose from fourth century scribes. In Old Testament times Latrun overlooked the valley of Aijalon where the sun stood still for Joshua while the Israelites defeated the Amorites (Joshua 10:12-14). Latrun gained its name from Le Toron des Chevaliers, the Tower of the (Crusader) Knights. Today Latrun is the site of three communities who work for peace in a troubled land. They are French-speaking Trappists, German-speaking Lutherans and an ecumenical commune of Jews, Christians and Muslims. A third Emmaus can be in the fellowship of the Lord's people as they seek friendship for the lonely, peace for the warring, and renewal for the earth.

The fourth proposed town is **Motza** which was settled, rebuilt by 800 Roman veterans after the First Jewish Revolt (66-70), and was renamed Colonia. It is mentioned by the Jewish historian Josephus. The site is about 3.5 miles/5.5 kilometres/ 30 stadia west of Jerusalem. In this case the accepted reading, which is the equivalent of 60 stadia, would represent the return trip to Emmaus from Jerusalem. Today it is a forgotten clump of trees and houses. A fourth Emmaus can be in the emptiness of life as the Lord's people cope with his seeming absence in an ever present bustling and bruising world.

Experiencing the Story

Perhaps this is a parable of earthly existence. As Frederick Buechner suggests, Emmaus is 'the place where he (Jesus) comes' and 'the place where we spend much of our lives, you and I, the place that we go to in order to escape.'[2] Inhabitants of Planet Earth may have a different Emmaus but they have the same Lord. History intersects with geography at Emmaus. The point of the story of the Emmaus Road is that Jesus meets us, reveals himself, and empowers us.

On the road to el-Qubeibeh in the experience of communal worship, or on the road to Abu Ghosh in the beauty of a holy place, or on the road to Latrun in the fellowship of the peacemakers, or on the road to Motza in the forsakenness of life, we can encounter Jesus and our hearts can burn within us. Emmaus is the time when we find our hearts 'strangely warmed' as did John Wesley on May 24, 1738.[3] Jesus makes the difference to the inhabitants of Planet Earth when his history intersects with our geography.

---

[2] Frederick Buechner, *The Magnificent Defeat*, p. 86.

[3] The story of Wesley's conversion is told in many places. For example, Justo L. Gonzalez, *The Story of Christianity*, 2:212 quotes Wesley's Journal. William Barclay translates *'Were not our hearts burning within us?'* as *'Were our hearts not strangely warmed?'*

Malcolm Muggeridge (1903-1990), formerly an agnostic journalist and latterly a Christian convert, experienced the story in an unforgettable manner. Muggeridge says,

> The road to Emmaus, walking along which with a friend I found myself living unforgettably through the experiences of the two travellers who took the same road shortly after the Crucifixion ... So much so that thenceforth I have never doubted that, wherever the walk and whoever the wayfarers, there is always, as on that other occasion on the road to Emmaus, a third presence ready to emerge from the shadows and fall in step along the dusty, stony way.[4]

Another person to experience the story of the Emmaus road was Jimmy Carter who served four years as President of the United States but failed to win a second term in the 1980 presidential election. His biographer Randall Balmer draws a parallel with the New Testament narratives of crucifixion and resurrection. Balmer tells of 'Carter's transformation from the ashes of political annihilation in 1980 to elder statesman, world-renowned humanitarian, and winner of the Nobel Peace Prize.'[5] Carter in his autobiography acknowledges the influence of Eloy Cruz, a Cuban-American Baptist pastor in Brooklyn, New York during a 'pioneer mission' in the late 1960s. Cruz's words remained with Carter all his days, namely, 'You only have to have two loves in your life: for God, and for the person in front of you at any particular time.'[6]

---

[4] Malcolm Muggeridge cited by Stephen Neill, *Jesus Through Many Eyes*, p. 195 n. 45.

[5] Randall Balmer, *Redeemer The Life of Jimmy Carter*, p. 162.

[6] Jimmy Carter, *A Full Life Reflections at Ninety*, p. 96.

Reflection

Think about experiences of worship, beauty, fellowship, and even forsakenness.

Prayer

Lord, you were the stranger on the road. Let our hearts burn within us in our experiences of worship, beauty, fellowship, and even forsakenness. Amen.

Part 4: Signs in John's Gospel

A Prayer for Readers of John's Gospel[1]

Living God of John's Good News about Jesus, we thank you for Jesus, the high flying eagle and the eternal contemporary. Raise us up on the wings of the high flying eagle and give us real life through our eternal contemporary. Let the light of Jesus, the true and living way, shine upon us. Amen.

---

[1] Doug Rowston, *A Bird's Eye View of the Bible Second Edition*, p. 155.

19   A Wedding

On the third day there was a wedding in Cana of Galilee, and the mother of Jesus was there. Jesus and his disciples had also been invited to the wedding. When the wine gave out, the mother of Jesus said to him, 'They have no wine.' And Jesus said to her, 'Woman, what concern is that to you and to me? My hour has not yet come.' His mother said to the servants, 'Do whatever he tells you.' Now standing there were six stone water jars for the Jewish rites of purification, each holding twenty or thirty gallons. Jesus said to them, 'Fill the jars with water.' And they filled them up to the brim. He said to them, 'Now draw some out, and take it to the chief steward.' So they took it. When the steward tasted the water that had become wine, and did not know where it came from (though the servants who had drawn the water knew), the steward called the bridegroom and said to him, 'Everyone serves the good wine first, and then the inferior wine after the guests have become drunk. But you have kept the good wine until now.' Jesus did this, the first of his signs, in Cana of Galilee, and revealed his glory; and his disciples believed in him.
(John 2:1-11; Aland, *Synopsis* # 22)

Telling the Story

The setting of the first sign is a wedding in Cana of Galilee. Mary, her son Jesus, and his disciples are there. Mary turns to Jesus in a moment of social embarrassment. *'They have no wine.'* The supply of wine has dried up. But Jesus refuses his mother's implied request to do something about it immediately by saying, *'Woman, what concern is that to you and to me? My hour has not yet come.'* Even so, Mary advises the servants to do whatever Jesus tells them to do.

The actual sign occurs after Jesus tells the servants to fill six stone jars with water. These jars are designed to be used in Jewish ritual cleansing and can hold about 20 to 30 gallons (80 to 120 litres) each. Jesus tells the servants, *'Fill the jars with water.'* When the jars are full, Jesus says, *'Now draw some out, and take it to the chief steward.'* He tastes the water turned into wine and being ignorant of the source, brings the wine to the attention of the bridegroom saying, *'Everyone serves the good wine first, and then the inferior wine after the guests have become drunk. But you have kept the good wine until now.'* This is a superior wine! How can this be served last?

This first sign of Jesus is substantiated by people who are unaware of what has happened. But there are people who move beyond the greatness of the gift to the greatness of the giver. Jesus reveals his splendour and his disciples perceive the significance of Jesus. John records, *Jesus did this, the first of his signs, in Cana of Galilee, and revealed his glory; and his disciples believed in him.*

Interpreting the Story

The incident is located at the beginning of the Gospel's Book of Signs in chapters 2 to 12. As we shall see, in each sign the readers are directed to respond to the glory of God in the person of Jesus. Water is turned to wine, a royal official's son is saved from death, a lame man is healed, five thousand are fed, Jesus crosses the lake, a man born blind receives his sight, and a dead man is restored to life.

At the wedding in Cana Jesus says, *'My hour has not yet come.'* Throughout the Fourth Gospel there are intriguing references to the hour of Jesus. In the temple *no one laid hands on him, because his hour had not yet come* and *no one arrested him, because his hour had not yet come. (John 7:30; 8:20)* Jesus speaks with disciples, *'The hour has come for the Son of Man to be glorified ... it is for this reason that I have come to this hour.'(John 12:23, 27)* Before the Passover J*esus knew that his hour had come to depart from this world and go to the Father. (John 13:1)* In the Gospel's Book of Glory in chapters 13 to 20 after the Farewell Discourse Jesus prays, *'Father, the hour has come; glorify your Son so that the Son may glorify you.'(John 17:1)*

Now the wedding at Cana features water and wine and one is reminded of Jesus' conversation with a Samaritan woman about the contrast between water drawn from Jacob's well and the living water Jesus offers. As Jesus said to her, *'Everyone who drinks of this water will be thirsty again, but those who drink of the water that I will give them will never be thirsty. The water that I will give will become in them a spring of water gushing up to eternal life.' (John 4:13-14)* The water in the six stone jars at Cana is limited to the Jewish rites of purification, limited like the water at Jacob's well.

One is also reminded of other references to wine in Old and New Testaments. In Isaiah the Old Testament prophet promises, *On this mountain the LORD of hosts will make for all peoples a feast of rich food, a feast of well-aged wines, of rich food filled with marrow, of well-aged wines strained clear. (Isaiah 25:6)* In the Gospels Jesus himself says, *'And no one puts new wine into old wineskins; otherwise, the wine will burst the skins, and the wine is lost, and so are the skins; but one puts new wine into fresh wineskins.' (Mark 2:22)*

One is finally reminded of the symbolism of the wedding in the visions of the last book of the Bible. *'Hallelujah! For the Lord our God the Almighty reigns. Let us rejoice and exult and give him the glory, for the marriage of the Lamb has come, and his bride has made herself ready; to her it has been granted to be clothed with fine linen, bright and pure.'(Revelation 19:6-8)* The common elements of the wedding, the water and the wine are joy and life.

Of course, one is confronted with the sceptic who refuses to accept that water was turned into wine by the power of God in Christ. As C.S. Lewis argued quite cleverly, in the natural order of things God makes wine, but it takes time as vines grow and grapes develop with rain, soil and sunlight. The miracle of turning water into wine is what God is always doing, but at the wedding in Cana the process is short circuited. 'The Miracle consists in the short cut; but the event to which it leads is the usual one.'[1]

Experiencing the Story

It is helpful to remember the words of an 'I am' saying of Jesus. We may well experience the reality of the story of Jesus turning water into wine by mulling over Jesus' identification with the true vine, the giver of the true wine. *'I am the true vine, and my Father is the vine-grower. He removes every branch in me that bears no fruit. Every branch that bears fruit he prunes to make it bear more fruit ... I am the vine, you are the branches. Those who abide in me and I in them bear much fruit, because apart from me you can do nothing.' (John 15:1-2, 5)*[2]

---

[1] C.S. Lewis, *Miracles*, p. 164.

[2] See Doug Rowston, *Jesus and Life*, pp. 39-42.

This 'I am' saying does three things. First, it describes Jesus as the whole vine, the fruitful vine, with its branches, the Jews and Greeks who abide in him. Second, it defines who are followers of Jesus. The disciples are the branches and must abide in Jesus by faith. Third, it provides the promise of Jesus for his followers. Jesus says that he will cut off dead branches and cut clean living branches so that they produce much fruit. As C.K. Barrett notes, the passage about the true vine in John 15:1-17 'is speaking of the union of believers with Christ, apart from whom they can do nothing. This union, originating in his initiative and sealed by his death on their behalf, is completed by the believers' responsive love and obedience, and is the essence of Christianity.'[3]

An ancient Jewish prayer gives thanks for the fruit of the vine: 'Blessed are You, Lord, our God, King of the Universe, who creates the fruit of the vine.' In addition, a second century Christian prayer gives thanks for the cup at the Lord's Supper: 'We thank you, our Father, for the holy vine of David, your child, which you have revealed through Jesus, your child. To you be glory forever.'[4] Whether it's at the dinner table or at the communion table, we may experience the goodness of God the Creator and Redeemer.

An oft told tale is about a converted alcoholic. His workmates kidding him about his new found faith asked, 'You don't believe what you read in the Bible, do you? For example, how on earth could Jesus turn water into wine? That's just a made up story, isn't it?' The new convert thought hard and said,

---

[3] C.K. Barrett, *The Gospel According To St. John*, p. 470.

[4] The Didache 9:2 (*The Library of Christian Classics*, 1:175)

'Whether he turned water into wine or not, all I know is that in my home he has turned beer into furniture!'

Reflection

Think about the gifts of God we receive in our daily living.

Prayer

Lord, help us to be thankful for your gifts at the dinner table and your gift of Jesus at the communion table. Amen.

20 A Royal Official

Then he came again to Cana in Galilee where he had changed the water into wine. Now there was a royal official whose son lay ill in Capernaum. When he heard that Jesus had come from Judea to Galilee, he went and begged him to come down and heal his son, for he was at the point of death. Then Jesus said to him, 'Unless you see signs and wonders you will not believe.' The official said to him, 'Sir, come down before my little boy dies.' Jesus said to him, 'Go; your son will live.' The man believed the word that Jesus spoke to him and started on his way. As he was going down, his slaves met him and told him that his child was alive. So he asked them the hour when he began to recover, and they said to him, 'Yesterday at one in the afternoon the fever left him.' The father realised that this was the hour when Jesus had said to him, 'Your son will live.' So he himself believed, along with his whole household. Now this was the second sign that Jesus did after coming from Judea to Galilee.
(John 4:46-54; Aland, *Synopsis* # 85)

Telling the Story

Jesus is in Cana where he did the first sign. A royal official comes about 24 to 32 kilometres (15 to 20 miles) from the lakeshore town of Capernaum up to Cana somewhere in the Galilean hills. We know that the ruins of Capernaum are on the northern edge of Lake Galilee but we are indebted to church tradition for a possible location of Cana.[1] He begs Jesus to come to Capernaum and heal his dying son. Jesus addresses the onlookers, *'Unless you* [plural] *see signs and wonders you* [plural] *will not believe.'* The official persists, *'Sir, come down before my little boy dies.'* Jesus responds, *'Go; your son will live.'*

Obediently trusting *the word that Jesus spoke to him* the official starts on his way back home. Next day on his way

---

[1] See Peter Walker, *In the Steps of Jesus*, pp. 37, 69-70.

home, it is a taxing journey, his household slaves meet him with good news. His child is alive! So he asks them when did his little boy start to get well. They say, *'Yesterday at one in the afternoon the fever left him.'* The father realises that it was at the time Jesus said, *'Your son will live.'* The official expresses his faith in the company of his household. *Now this was the second sign that Jesus did after coming from Judea to Galilee.*

Interpreting the Story

As Alan Culpepper comments, 'The story drives home the theme: Jesus gives life to those who believe in him.'[2] First, the Fourth Evangelist emphasises the gift of life. The narrative includes the promise of Jesus to the official, *'Go; your son will live.'* As a result, it is noted, the official *believed the word that Jesus spoke to him.* The narrative concludes on the next day with the official's realization of the timing of his son's improvement. It was when Jesus said, 'Your son will live.' As a result, it is noted again, the official *himself believed, along with his whole household.* At the beginning and end of the Gospel there are significant references to the life given by God through Jesus: *In him* [the Word] *was life, and the life was the light of all people* and *Through believing you may have life in his* [Jesus'] *name. (John 1:4; 20:31)*

Second, the Fourth Evangelist stresses the importance of belief. As William Hull points out,[3] the narrative distinguishes three kinds of belief. One negative kind is belief founded upon

---

[2] R. Alan Culpepper, *The Gospel and Letters of John*, p. 146.

[3] William E. Hull, 'John', *The Broadman Bible Commentary*, 9:259.

seeing *signs and wonders*. Such belief would require the need for a miracle to produce trust in God. Jesus tells the onlookers not to go that way. Another kind of belief is positive: the father in the story *believed the word that Jesus spoke to him and started on his way.* The man's belief is not by sight but is insightful. A third and most significant kind of belief is a further development. *So he himself believed, along with his whole household.* The official's insight is verified by the powerful impact of the words of Jesus in new life for the young boy and in new faith for the official's household.

Experiencing the Story

Once again it is helpful to recall one of the 'I am' sayings of Jesus so we can experience even more deeply of the meaning of Jesus giving life to the official's young boy which reveals Jesus as the true and living way. *'I am the way, and the truth, and the life. No one comes to the Father except through me. If you know me, you will know my Father also. From now on you do know him and have seen him.' (John 14:6-7)*[4]

This 'I am' saying does three things. First, it gives a description of Jesus. Jesus is the way, the means of access to the meaning of existence. Jesus is the way because he is the truth, that is to say, fidelity and reality. Jesus is the way because he is the life, he brings divine light into human darkness. Second, it states the requirement for followers of Jesus. They come to the Father through Jesus. Third, it provides the promise of Jesus for his followers, by knowing Jesus they come to know God.

---

[4] See Doug Rowston, *Jesus and Life*, pp. 35-38.

On the western wall of the church I belong to is an honour roll of our missionaries. The first name on the list is Ellen Arnold. She was a young school teacher who went as a missionary from Adelaide to Bengal. She took the way of persistence, service and sacrifice in following Jesus. She worked in Faridpur, Mymensingh, Pabna, Bera, and Ataikola from 1882 to 1931. I had the privilege of standing next to her gravestone in Bangladesh. It bears the Bengali inscription: 'Jesus said, 'I am the Way, the Truth, and the Life.' Ellen Arnold walked this Way, taught this Truth, and lived this Life.' In a very real sense Ellen Arnold experienced Jesus giving life to the people among whom she lived and worked in Bengal.

Reflection

Think about people who need our formal and informal prayers.

Prayer

Lord, help us to be faithful in our prayers for people we spend time with, for the community of faith, for leaders of our world, and for members of our own family. Amen.

21   A Lame Man

After this there was a festival of the Jews, and Jesus went up to Jerusalem. Now in Jerusalem by the Sheep Gate there is a pool, called in Hebrew [That is, Aramaic] *Beth-zatha, which has five porticoes. In these lay many invalids—blind, lame, and paralysed. One man was there who had been ill for thirty-eight years. When Jesus saw him lying there and knew that he had been there a long time, he said to him, 'Do you want to be made well?' The sick man answered him, 'Sir, I have no one to put me into the pool when the water is stirred up; and while I am making my way, someone else steps down ahead of me.' Jesus said to him, 'Stand up, take your mat and walk.' At once the man was made well, and he took up his mat and began to walk. Now that day was a sabbath. So the Jews said to the man who had been cured, 'It is the sabbath; it is not lawful for you to carry your mat.' But he answered them, 'The man who made me well said to me, 'Take up your mat and walk.'' They asked him, 'Who is the man who said to you, 'Take it up and walk'?' Now the man who had been healed did not know who it was, for Jesus had disappeared in the crowd that was there. Later Jesus found him in the temple and said to him, 'See, you have been made well! Do not sin any more, so that nothing worse happens to you.' The man went away and told the Jews that it was Jesus who had made him well. Therefore the Jews started persecuting Jesus, because he was doing such things on the sabbath. But Jesus answered them, 'My Father is still working, and I also am working.' For this reason the Jews were seeking all the more to kill him, because he was not only breaking the sabbath, but was also calling God his own Father, thereby making himself equal to God.*
(John 5:1-18; Aland, *Synopsis* # 141)

Telling the Story

A valuable monograph is *The Rediscovery of Bethesda* by Joachim Jeremias. It provides useful information about the location of this story. At an unnamed Jewish festival Jesus is in Jerusalem and is near the Sheep Gate where there is a twin pool called Bethzatha in Aramaic, or Bethesda in Hebrew. The Hebrew form Bethesda can be interpreted as 'House of Mercy'.[1]

---

[1] Joachim Jeremias, *The Rediscovery of Bethesda*, p. 12.

Four porticoes surrounded the twin pools and a fifth portico was in the middle of the pools.

A reconstruction of Bethesda as it was in the time of Jesus[2]

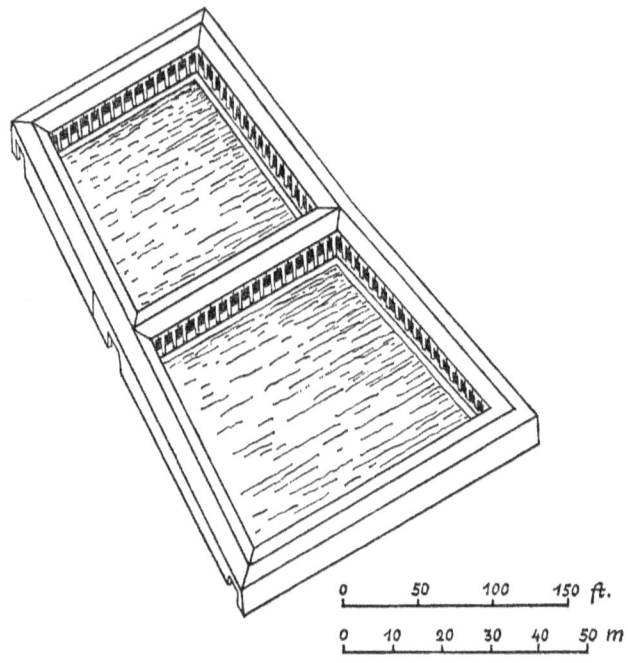

The middle portico or colonnade provided room for needy people to sit and lay down. Apparently the sick including blind, lame, and paralysed awaited the stirring of the waters before stepping into the twin pool. Among many invalids Jesus comes across a long time resident of the area. Jesus asks him, *'Do you want to be made well?'* After the sick man offers excuses, Jesus challenges him, *'Stand up, take your mat and walk.'*

---

[2] Ibid., pp. 26-27. The northern pool measured approximately 169 x 131 feet (51.5 x 39.9 metres); the southern pool measured approximately 202 x 160 feet (61.6 x 48.8 metres).

Surprisingly, there is no mention of belief on the part of the man. However, the man is immediately made well, takes up his mat and begins to walk. Then the Jewish religious leaders confront the man with the words, *'It is the sabbath; it is not lawful for you to carry your mat.'* They are determined to criticise the man who has been cured for working on the sabbath, the Jewish day of rest.

In the Mishnah, the second century commentary on the Jewish Law, there is a list of thirty-nine main classes of work prohibited on the day of rest. The list is as follows:

he who sows and ploughs and reaps and binds; he who threshes and winnows and fans; he who sifts and kneads and bakes; he who shears wool and bleaches it and combs and dyes and spins; he who weaves and draws and twists and separates two threads; he who ties and unties a knot and sews two stitches and tears apart to sew two stitches; he who hunts and kills and skins a gazelle; he who salts it and dresses its skin and scrapes and cuts it; he who writes two letters and rubs out against write two letters; he who builds and pulls down; he who lights a fire and puts it out; he who strikes with a hammer; he who carries from one place to another.[3]

The man who has been cured passes the blame on to his healer who is unknown to him. When he encounters Jesus in the temple, he is told by Jesus, *'See, you have been made well! Do not sin any more, so that nothing worse happens to you.'* Afterwards the man goes and informs the Jewish religious leaders that it is Jesus who healed him. So they now criticise Jesus for working on the sabbath and in the face of their criticism Jesus replies, *'My Father is still working, and I also am working.'* Jesus links his work with God's work of creation.

---

[3] Eduard Lohse, *'sabbaton'*, *Theological Dictionary of the New Testament*, 7:12.

Therefore Jesus is criticised not only for breaking the rules of the sabbath but also for suggesting that God is his Father.

Interpreting the Story

The story of the man at Bethesda is best interpreted by considering the following discourse about the authority of Jesus (John 5:19-29) and the witnesses to Jesus (John 5:30-47).

First, the authority of Jesus is highlighted by the parable of the apprentice son.[4] *'Very truly, I tell you, the Son can do nothing on his own, but only what he sees the Father doing; for whatever the Father does, the Son does likewise. The Father loves the Son and shows him all that he himself is doing.' (John 5:19-20)* As a young boy in the carpenter's shop, Jesus would have learned from, imitated, and appreciated his earthly father Joseph. Jesus tells this parable to point towards the unity of action between himself and his heavenly Father and the complete dependence of himself upon his heavenly Father.

The authority of Jesus is reinforced by the references to the power of life and judgement shared with God. *'Indeed, just as the Father raises the dead and gives them life, so also the Son gives life to whomever he wishes. The Father judges no one but has given all judgement to the Son.' (John 5:22-23)* People can listen to Jesus, believe in him, and pass from existence without God to life with God. *'Very truly, I tell you, anyone who hears my word and believes him who sent me has eternal life, and does not come under judgement, but has passed from death to life.' (John 5:24)*

---

[4] See Doug Rowston, *Things that Jesus said*, pp. 121-126.

Second, the witnesses to Jesus include John the Baptist, the works of Jesus, and the scriptures. First, John the Baptist *'testified to the truth ... and was a burning and shining lamp.' (5:33, 35)* Second, Jesus refers to his works,*'The works that the Father has given me to complete ... testify on my behalf that the Father has sent me.' (5:36)* Third, the scriptures are also witnesses. As Jesus says, *'You search the scriptures because you think that in them you have eternal life; and it is they that testify on my behalf.' (5:39)*

Experiencing the Story

Are there times in our lives when the Lord comes to us and asks, 'Do you want to be made well?' Once again it is helpful to recall the words of another 'I am' saying of Jesus. Accordingly we can experience the reality of the story of Jesus giving health to the lame man at Bethesda by meditating on Jesus' identification with the gate or door to life. *'I am the gate. Whoever enters by me will be saved, and will come in and go out and find pasture. The thief comes only to steal and kill and destroy. I came that they may have life, and have it abundantly.' (John 10:9-10)*[5]

This 'I am' saying gives three things. First, it describes Jesus. Jesus contrasts himself with the thief and calls himself the gate for the sheep to enter into the sheepfold. Second, it requires something of followers of Jesus. Jesus asks all who want to follow him to enter through the true gate to find safety, freedom and sustenance. Third, it promises something to his

---

[5] See Doug Rowston, *Jesus and Life*, pp. 19-22.

followers. Jesus gives all who decide to follow him life in all its abundance.

Life in all its fullness is best exemplified by the life story of Louie Zamperini.[6] After transforming himself from a juvenile delinquent into a promising athlete he gained fame as a nineteen year old runner at the Berlin Olympics in 1936. Although he didn't win a medal he ran the fastest lap in the 5000 metre final. Louie was looking forward to doing better in a shorter distance at the Tokyo Olympics in 1940. However, war intervened and Louie found himself in a succession of challenging situations. He joined the US Air Force, became a bombardier, flew missions over the Pacific, was shot down by the Japanese, drifted 3200 kilometres (2000 miles) in a raft, became a prisoner of war, suffered terribly in POW camps, and somehow survived.

Back home in 1946 he married an upper class girl. Unable to resume athletics due to wartime injuries, he drank alcohol excessively and suffered horrible nightmares of his wartime imprisonment. Even though he was treated as a hero, his life spun out of control. In 1949 at his wife's insistence they went to the Los Angeles Billy Graham Crusade. Louie was not convinced of what he heard but Cynthia was still insistent and they went again. That night Louie remembered a prayer that he had not kept on the raft in the Pacific, *'If you save me, I will*

---

[6] Laura Hillenbrand, *Unbroken*.

serve you forever.[7] After the meeting Louie returned home and dispensed with things that were part of his old life. The next day he started reading the Bible which he had received as an airman. It had been sent home to his mother when he was missing presumed dead. Louie learned the truth of the words, *'I came that they may have life, and have it abundantly.'*

Reflection

Think about the opportunities given to us for meaningful change and development.

Prayer

Lord, help us to avail ourselves of your guidance that comes in worship and work so that we may be the people you want us to be. Amen.

---

[7] Ibid., p. 382.

22 A Large Crowd

After this Jesus went to the other side of the Sea of Galilee, also called the Sea of Tiberias. A large crowd kept following him, because they saw the signs that he was doing for the sick. 3 Jesus went up the mountain and sat down there with his disciples. Now the Passover, the festival of the Jews, was near. When he looked up and saw a large crowd coming toward him, Jesus said to Philip, 'Where are we to buy bread for these people to eat?' He said this to test him, for he himself knew what he was going to do. Philip answered him, 'Six months' wages would not buy enough bread for each of them to get a little.' One of his disciples, Andrew, Simon Peter's brother, said to him, 'There is a boy here who has five barley loaves and two fish. But what are they among so many people?' Jesus said, 'Make the people sit down.' Now there was a great deal of grass in the place; so they sat down, about five thousand in all. Then Jesus took the loaves, and when he had given thanks, he distributed them to those who were seated; so also the fish, as much as they wanted. When they were satisfied, he told his disciples, 'Gather up the fragments left over, so that nothing may be lost.' So they gathered them up, and from the fragments of the five barley loaves, left by those who had eaten, they filled twelve baskets. When the people saw the sign that he had done, they began to say, 'This is indeed the prophet who is to come into the world.' When Jesus realised that they were about to come and take him by force to make him king, he withdrew again to the mountain by himself.
(John 6:1-15; compare Matthew 14:13-21; Mark 6:32-44; Luke 9:10b-17; Aland, *Synopsis* # 146)

Telling the Story

It is around Passover time. *Now the Passover, the festival of the Jews, was near.* The people would recall the Great Escape from Egypt by their ancestors under the leadership of Moses. The people are probably on the eastern shore of the Lake as they look for Jesus. *Jesus went to the other side of the Sea of Galilee* and *went up the mountain and sat down there with his disciples.* Would the people also recall that Moses received divine revelation on Mount Sinai and taught his disciples below Mount Sinai? Then Jesus sees the large crowd and says to Philip, *'Where are we to buy bread for these people to eat?'* He is testing Philip who acknowledges, *'Six months' wages* [literally *Two hundred denarii*[1]] *would not buy enough bread for each of them to get a little.'* Another disciple, Andrew, says to Jesus, *'There is a boy here who has five barley loaves and two fish. But what are they among so many people?'* Then Jesus says, *'Make the people sit down.'* It is a grassy place which is comfortable for reclining or sitting. Passover time is in the northern spring so there would be fresh grass.

Jesus takes the loaves and the fishes, gives thanks for them, distributes them to the people who are seated, and the crowd has as much as they desire. After the people have had their fill, Jesus tells his disciples, *'Gather up the fragments left over, so that nothing may be lost.'* In gathering the fragments the disciples fill twelve baskets. Would the crowd now recall the twelve tribes of the ancient people of God? Is Jesus the fulfilment of ancient prophecy? Moses had said, *'The LORD your God will raise up for you a prophet like me from among your own people; you shall heed such a prophet.'* (Deuteronomy 18:15) Indeed, God had said to Moses, *'I will raise up for them a prophet like you from among their own people; I will put my words in the mouth of the prophet, who shall speak to them everything that I command.'* (Deuteronomy 18:18) The people are recognising that Jesus has done a sign and are saying, *'This is indeed the prophet who is to come into the world.'* But Jesus, resisting the will of the crowd to crown him as an earthly ruler, goes back *to the mountain by himself.*

---

[1] The NRSV footnote explains: ' the denarius was the usual day's wage for a labourer.'

Interpreting the Story

The miracle of the feeding of the large crowd is the only miracle of Jesus which is told in all four Gospels. There are four interpretations of the story.

Matthew notes before the feeding that Jesus *saw a great crowd; and he had compassion for them and cured their sick.* At the end of Matthew's account it says that *all ate and were filled.* In between are hints of the coming climax in the ministry of Jesus. Both Matthew 14:13-21 (The Feeding of the Five Thousand) and 26:20-29 (The Last Supper) have obvious parallels: evening time, sitting down, taking bread, blessing the food, breaking bread, giving to disciples, and eating.[2] Matthew's version of the miracle, like Mark's, has themes of compassion, completeness and communion.

Mark gives probably the earliest version of the story which Matthew abbreviated. Before the feeding Mark mentions at length the compassion of Jesus for the crowd, *because they were like sheep without a shepherd*, and connects it with teaching. Alan Culpepper draws attention to three features in Mark's account when Jesus orders all *to sit down in **groups** on the **green** grass* and they do so *in **groups** of hundreds and of fifties.*[3] The first word translated *groups* had connotations of parties of people eating together in Greco Roman society.[4] The second word translated *groups* is literally *garden plot, garden*

---

[2] Dale C. Allison, Jr., *Matthew A Shorter Commentary*, p. 236.

[3] R. Alan Culpepper, *Mark*, pp. 210-11.

[4] Bauer et al., A *Greek-English Lexicon of the New Testament*, p. 959.

bed. 'From the lit(eral) sense "garden plot, garden bed" it is but a short step to ... **group by group** picturing the groups of people contrasted w(ith) the green grass.'[5] Finally Mark alone refers to springtime *green* grass, which is in accord with John's timing at Passover in springtime and is perhaps an allusion to Psalm 23:1-2, *The LORD is my shepherd, I shall not want. He makes me lie down in green pastures.*

Luke, also dependent on Mark, says that Jesus *welcomed* the crowds near Bethsaida *and spoke to them about the kingdom of God, and healed those who needed to be cured.* Luke and Mark report that Jesus says to the disciples, *'You give them something to eat.'* This command is like an incident in the story of the Old Testament prophet Elisha in 2 Kings 4:42-44. Howard Marshall comments, 'As in the OT story, so here a conversation follows in which human inability to fulfil such a command is expressed, and the way is prepared for the divine provision of plenty.'[6] Luke follows up the story of the miraculous feeding with the account of Peter's confession that Jesus is the Messiah. Luke's readers are faced with the question: *'But who do you say that I am?' (Luke 9:20)*

In John 6 the feeding of the five thousand is interpreted by the following discourse at the synagogue in Capernaum. The evangelist's record notes the living bread's source (6:25-34), nature (6:35-51) and reception (6:52-65). First, Jesus identifies its source, *'Very truly, I tell you, it was not Moses who gave you the bread from heaven, but it is my Father who gives you the*

---

[5] Ibid., p. 860.

[6] I. Howard Marshall, *The Gospel of Luke*, p. 360.

true bread from heaven.' (6:32) Second, Jesus discloses its nature, *'I am the living bread that came down from heaven. Whoever eats of this bread will live forever; and the bread that I will give for the life of the world is my flesh.' (6:51)* Third, in a vivid metaphor, Jesus refers to its reception, *'Those who eat my flesh and drink my blood abide in me, and I in them.' (6:56)* As William Hull suggests, 'The identity of giver and gift means that one cannot take something from Jesus without taking Jesus himself.'[7]

Experiencing the Story

An ancient Jewish prayer gives thanks for the bread of each day: 'Blessed are You, Lord, our God, who brings forth bread from the earth, who makes glad the hearts of your people.' In addition, a second century Christian prayer gives thanks for the bread at the Lord's Supper: 'We thank you, our Father, for the life and knowledge which you have revealed through Jesus, your child. To you be glory forever. As this piece [of bread] was scattered over the hills and then was brought together and made one, so let your Church be brought together from the ends of the earth into your Kingdom. For yours is the glory and the power through Jesus Christ forever.'[8] Whether it's at the dinner table or at the communion table, we may experience the goodness of God the Creator and Redeemer.

Furthermore, are there times in our lives when we ask ourselves, 'What can I do? I have so little in the face of something so big.' Once again it is helpful to recall the words

---

[7] William E. Hull, 'John', *The Broadman Bible Commentary*, 9:277.

[8] The Didache 9:3-4 (*The Library of Christian Classics*, 1:175).

of an 'I am' saying of Jesus. Accordingly, when we have very little we can enter into the reality of the story of Jesus feeding the large crowd with very little by meditating on Jesus' self identification with the bread of life. *'I am the bread of life. Whoever comes to me will never be hungry, and whoever believes in me will never be thirsty.' (John 6:35)*[9]

This 'I am' saying does three things. First, it describes Jesus as the bread which brings life. The bread of which he speaks is not a commodity, it is Jesus himself. Second, it requires something of followers of Jesus. Jesus asks all who want to follow him to come to him and to believe in him. It's a basic requirement that we should hunger and thirst for his life and teaching. Third, it promises something to his followers. Jesus promises them that they will never be hungry or thirsty. They will have all they need in him.

Previously we have mentioned the formidable figure of Ellen Arnold in the treatment of the second Johannine sign.[10] She had gone to East Bengal as a missionary from South Australia in 1882 but after eighteen months in Bengal, she was ordered home being too sick to stay. Convalescence was spent travelling the Australian colonies and New Zealand appealing for more workers. In 1885 Ellen recruited four other women in their twenties. At their commissioning in Flinders Street Baptist Church, Adelaide, Silas Mead called them the 'Five Barley Loaves.' Andrew says to Jesus in the story of Jesus feeding the large crowd with very little, *'There is a boy here who has **five barley loaves** and two fish. But what are they*

---

[9] See Doug Rowston, *Jesus and Life*, pp. 7-10.

[10] See p. 124 above.

among so many people?' In Australian Baptist Missions History Ellen Arnold, Alice Pappin, Ruth Wilkin, Marian Fuller, and Martha Plested are remembered as the 'Five Barley Loaves.' Starting with this small group of women Australian Baptists laboured in Bengal and after the second world war in New Guinea and Southern Africa and South East Asia. Much has been done with comparatively little.[11]

Reflection

Think about God's gifts to us that may be shared with others.

Prayer

Lord, encourage us to give, whether little or much, of what we have, in sharing your kind of life with people near and far. Amen.

---

[11] See Tony Cupit, et al., *From Five Barley Loaves.*

23 The Lake

When evening came, his disciples went down to the lake, got into a boat, and started across the lake to Capernaum. It was now dark, and Jesus had not yet come to them. The lake became rough because a strong wind was blowing. When they had rowed about three or four miles, they saw Jesus walking on the lake and coming near the boat, and they were terrified. But he said to them, 'It is I; do not be afraid.' Then they wanted to take him into the boat, and immediately the boat reached the land toward which they were going.
(John 6:16-21; compare Matthew 14:22-33; Mark 6:45-52; Aland, *Synopsis* # 147)

Telling the Story

According to John, after the five thousand are fed, Jesus withdraws to the hills by himself and in the evening his disciples get into a boat and begin rowing across the lake. It is dark, the lake is rough, the wind is blowing strongly, and the disciples are on their own as they make their way from Tiberias to Capernaum. Having rowed about three or four miles (five or six kilometres),[1] the disciples are frightened when they see Jesus *walking on the lake and coming near the boat*. Is this a parallel of Jesus walking 'by the seashore' when he met the seven disciples after the resurrection *by the Sea of Tiberias* in John 21:5? Or is it Jesus crossing the lake in an unusual way as two other evangelists seem to indicate by saying he was *walking on the sea* in Matthew 14:25-26 and Mark 6:48-49? However this matter is interpreted by readers, the boat is nearly at its destination. There are two points of interest here. On the one hand, Jesus is in command. Jesus says to the disciples, '*It is*

---

[1] Literally *about twenty five or thirty stadia*. A stade was a furlong or one eighth of a mile. See Bauer et al., A *Greek-English Lexicon of the New Testament*, p. 940.

I [literally *I am*]; *do not be afraid.'* On the other hand, the disciples are in need. All they want to do is to get him to join them in the boat. Finally, there may even be two miraculous events: the unusual coming of Jesus to the boat and the immediate arrival of the boat on land.

Interpreting the Story

In Matthew 14 and Mark 6 there are two other versions of a story about crossing the lake. In all three versions a miraculous feeding of a large crowd is accompanied by a miraculous crossing of the lake. Early readers of the Gospels would no doubt recall the words of the Psalmist: God *divided the sea and let them pass through it, and made the waters stand like a heap ... he rained down on them manna to eat, and gave them the grain of heaven. (Psalm 78: 13, 24)* As Alan Culpepper notes, 'Having fed people as Moses did in the wilderness, Jesus now performs a sea miracle, like the parting of the sea at the Exodus.'[2]

Interpreting the story does raise questions of historicity. For example, the venerable Scot says, 'The Greek is *epi tes thalasses* which is precisely the phrase used in *John 21:1*, where it means - it has never been questioned - that Jesus was walking on the seashore. That is what the phrase means in our passage, too.'[3] Although Mark followed by Matthew reported a walking on the lake, the focus of John's version is elsewhere. This does not mean that John does not accept that something

---

[2] R. Alan Culpepper, *The Gospel and Letters of John*, p. 157.

[3] William Barclay, *The Daily Study Bible: John,* 1:208.

miraculous happened, rather, 'John treats the scene as a divine epiphany centered in the expression *ego eimi* [Greek, to be translated *I am*] in vs. 20.'[4] In other words, John is saying that God, who reveals himself to Moses as *'I AM' (Exodus 3:14)*, is revealing himself in Jesus who, like Moses, feeds a large crowd and crosses the sea. An interesting suggestion has been made that the walking on the lake was originally a post-resurrection narrative. However this suggestion is judged, it is true to say with C.H. Dodd, 'It is the recognition of Jesus, unexpectedly present to his disciples in their need, that is the true centre of the story.'[5]

Experiencing the Story

Tom Wright suggests that this story provides helpful subject matter for meditation. In the face of the dark experiences of loss, the rough waves of the unexpected, the strong winds of tough times, the fears of the unknown, this story reminds us of Jesus. Wright comments, 'As we struggle to make our way through, sometimes we become aware of a presence with us, which may be more disturbing than comforting ... But if we listen, through the roar of the waves and the wind, we may hear the voice that says, "It's me - don't be afraid." '[6]

Another 'I am' saying also points to Jesus, *'I am the good shepherd. I know my own and my own know me, just as the Father knows me and I know the Father. And I lay down my life*

---

[4] Raymond E. Brown, *The Gospel of John,* 1:254.

[5] C.H. Dodd, *Historical Tradition in the Fourth Gospel,* p. 198.

[6] Tom Wright, *John for Everyone,* 1:77.

for the sheep.' (John 10:14-15)[7] With this saying we learn three things. First, there is a description of Jesus. By describing himself as the good shepherd he compares himself with past and present leaders. In feeding a large crowd and crossing the lake Jesus reveals the Great I AM and is greater than Moses. Second, there is a requirement made of followers of Jesus. Jesus implies that they need to get to know him and to experience his companionship. Third, there is a promise given to his followers. Jesus knows his sheep intimately and is willing to die to protect them.

Jonathan Edwards is an Englishman who came to fame in 1995 by breaking a ten year old world record for the triple jump at the World Championships. Yet he struggled to recapture his top form in this event. He 'failed' when he won the silver medal at the Atlanta Olympic Games in 1996. He faced injury and criticism. He struggled with expectations both as an athlete and as a follower of Jesus. Yet he endured and competed at the 2000 Sydney Olympics. On the day that Cathy Freeman won the Women's 400 metres and Michael Johnson won the Men's 400 metres, Jonathan Edwards won the gold medal in his specialty, the triple jump. His biographer Malcolm Folley said, 'Edwards' accomplishment was a stunning triumph for a man who never lost faith in his ability, and who kept his faith in God.' Edwards himself responded, 'It was everything for me to win the gold medal, and it was nothing. I am not defined by the fact I am Olympic champion. I am defined by God's love for me and my love for him; and my love for my family and their

---

[7] See Doug Rowston, *Jesus and Life*, pp. 23-28.

love for me. But as a Christian athlete I felt I had a debt of duty to give my all in pursuit of Olympic gold.'[8]

Reflection

Think about the rough waves and the strong winds of life that confront us.

Prayer

Lord, come to us in the tough times of life so that we may survive, even thrive, and help others to do so in similar circumstances. Amen.

---

[8] Malcolm Folley, *A Time To Jump*, pp. 364-365.

24 A Blind Man

As he walked along, he saw a man blind from birth. His disciples asked him, 'Rabbi, who sinned, this man or his parents, that he was born blind?' Jesus answered, 'Neither this man nor his parents sinned; he was born blind so that God's works might be revealed in him. We must work the works of him who sent me while it is day; night is coming when no one can work. As long as I am in the world, I am the light of the world.' When he had said this, he spat on the ground and made mud with the saliva and spread the mud on the man's eyes, saying to him, 'Go, wash in the pool of Siloam' (which means Sent). Then he went and washed and came back able to see. The neighbours and those who had seen him before as a beggar began to ask, 'Is this not the man who used to sit and beg?' Some were saying, 'It is he.' Others were saying, 'No, but it is someone like him.' He kept saying, 'I am the man.' But they kept asking him, 'Then how were your eyes opened?' He answered, 'The man called Jesus made mud, spread it on my eyes, and said to me, 'Go to Siloam and wash.' Then I went and washed and received my sight.' They said to him, 'Where is he?' He said, 'I do not know.'
(John 9:1-12; Aland, *Synopsis* # 248

Telling the Story

The above extract includes the opening scenes in this story of Jesus in John 9. At first, Jesus heals a man born blind by making a dirt or sand paste, spreading it on the man's eyes, and telling him to go and wash in the pool of Siloam.[1] When the man comes back seeing, his neighbours are staggered and question whether it is the same man. The man acknowledges his identity and describes how his sight was restored by *'the man called Jesus'.* But he doesn't know where Jesus is.

Further scenes in this story include the questioning of the man by the Pharisees (9:13-17), questioning of his parents by the

---

[1] My wife and I saw the beginning of excavations of stone steps leading into the ruins of the Siloam Pool in January 2005. See *Biblical Archaeology Review 200th Issue*, vol. 35 nos. 4/5, pp. 90-91.

Pharisees (9:18-23), and more questioning of the man by the Pharisees (9:24-34). In the process the man blurts out, *'He is a prophet.'* However, his parents while acknowledging their son claim ignorance of his healer. They say this for fear the religious leaders will excommunicate any who confess that Jesus is *the Messiah*. By way of contrast, their son says to his inquisitors, *'One thing I do know, that though I was blind, now I see.'* By this he is prepared to infer that Jesus is *'from God'*.

Finally, Jesus questions the man (9:35-38) and the Pharisees question Jesus (9:39-41). On the one hand, the man accepts Jesus' own claim to be *'the Son of Man'*. As we have noted in the treatment of Matthew's version of the healing of a paralysed man,[2] the reference to the Son of Man recalls the vision of Daniel 7:13-14 concerning the judge at the end of time. This formerly blind man confesses, *'Lord, I believe.'* On the other hand, the Pharisees are a sad case with Jesus summing up the situation, *'I came into this world for judgement so that those who do not see may see, and those who do see may become blind.'*

Interpreting the Story

Throughout the Gospel of John there are contrasting responses to Jesus. Of particular interest in this story are two things, one inside and another outside.[3]

---

[2] See p. 29 above.

[3] See R. Alan Culpepper, *Anatomy of the Fourth Gospel*, pp. 139-40.

First, within the story the man proceeds from physical blindness to physical sight and spiritual insight and the Pharisees move from supposed sightfulness to spiritual blindness. At the beginning, the man born blind is in dire straits; his blindness is seen as a consequence of his or his parents' sin. The religious opponents of Jesus cannot understand how a supposed healer who breaks the sabbath can be from God, let alone perform such a sign as to make the blind to see. At the end, the man has received both sight and insight while the Pharisees sink to the depths of spiritual blindness and wilful sinfulness.

Second, there is a striking contrast between the blind man of John 9 and the lame man of John 5. The blind man learns from his encounter with Jesus. As instructed he goes to the pool of Siloam, rejoices in his recovery of sight, and then acknowledges the identity of his healer. All the while he is not put off by the Pharisees who don't want to accept his testimony and wish to drive him out. He accepts the assurance of Jesus, believes in him, and falls down in worship. On the other hand, the lame man at the pool of Bethesda has to be challenged about his willingness to be made well. When he is, he has the sense to take up his mat and walk. However, when he learns the identity of his healer he reports back to the Jewish religious leaders with resulting persecution for Jesus the sabbath breaker and supposed blasphemer. The previously lame man does not come to faith in Jesus; he just disappears from the scene.

Experiencing the Story

As Ben Witherington observes, the story of the blind man is 'an apt exegesis'[4] of words in the opening to the Fourth Gospel: *In him was life, and the life was the light of all people. The light shines in the darkness, and the darkness did not overcome it ... He was in the world, and the world came into being through him; yet the world did not know him. He came to what was his own, and his own people did not accept him. (John 1:4-5, 10-11)*

The blind man illustrates an 'I am' saying of Jesus, namely, *'I am the light of the world. Whoever follows me will never walk in darkness but will have the light of life.' (John 8:12)*[5] First, the blind man comes to know Jesus as the light of his world. In terms of the exodus, Jesus is the pillar of fire leading God's people out of the land of sin and death into the land of righteousness and life. Second, the blind man receives the promise of Jesus to acquire light and experience life. In terms of the return from exile, Jesus shapes a people who are to bring light to the nations and to open the eyes of the blind. Third, the blind man meets the requirement of Jesus to reflect the light and to share the life of his Lord. Jesus is the light to be followed. If we live in darkness, we miss the growth, the health, the goodness which light brings. If the man born blind in John 9 had not followed the light, he would have missed the power and truth of God. In fact, he did follow the light. His last recorded words are *'Lord, I believe.'* As William Hull says, 'Having discovered how dangerous it can be to see the world

---

[4] Ben Witherington III, *John's Wisdom*, p. 181.

[5] See Doug Rowston, *Jesus and Life*, pp. 11-14.

for what it is, he now learned how redemptive it can be to see Jesus for who he is.'[6]

As my family drove through the Adelaide hills when my children were young, they used to enjoy seeing the lights of the city of Adelaide, lights which we called 'Fairyland'. They lit up the dark of the surrounding suburbs and made a lovely view, especially at the end of a long journey home from visiting relatives in Melbourne. When Jesus told his disciples that he was the light of the world he was giving a meaningful word picture about finding the way in the midst of a dark and threatening world.

Reflection

Think about times in which darkness seems to overcome light in our world.

Prayer

Lord, when we see a dark and threatening world for what it is, help us to see Jesus for who he is, the light and life of all that is. Amen.

---

[6] William E. Hull, 'John', *The Broadman Bible Commentary*, 9:301.

25   Dead Lazarus

Then Jesus, again greatly disturbed, came to the tomb. It was a cave, and a stone was lying against it. Jesus said, 'Take away the stone.' Martha, the sister of the dead man, said to him, 'Lord, already there is a stench because he has been dead four days.' Jesus said to her, 'Did I not tell you that if you believed, you would see the glory of God?' So they took away the stone. And Jesus looked upward and said, 'Father, I thank you for having heard me. I knew that you always hear me, but I have said this for the sake of the crowd standing here, so that they may believe that you sent me.' 43 When he had said this, he cried with a loud voice, 'Lazarus, come out!' The dead man came out, his hands and feet bound with strips of cloth, and his face wrapped in a cloth. Jesus said to them, 'Unbind him, and let him go.'
(John 11:38-44; Aland, Synopsis # 259)

Telling the Story

The extract concludes the account of the raising of Lazarus in John 11. The earlier part of the story tells of the request made by two sisters for Jesus to come to Bethany because their brother is ill. Jesus waits for two days before discussing the situation with his disciples. Then as they leave for Bethany in Judea, he explains, *'Our friend Lazarus has fallen asleep, but I am going there to awaken him.' (11:11)* His disciples think that Lazarus will be all right. Jesus corrects their misunderstanding of the metaphor and elaborates, *'Lazarus is dead. For your sake I am glad I was not there, so that you may believe. But let us go to him.' (11:14)* By the time of their arrival at Bethany, Lazarus has been in his tomb for four days.

Martha, one of his sisters, meets Jesus and criticises him for his delayed arrival. Jesus assures her, *'Your brother will rise again.' (11:23)* Martha affirms the popular Jewish expectation,*'I know that he will rise again in the resurrection on the last day.' (11:24)* Then Jesus brings future expectation into present experience. *'I am the resurrection and the life. Those who believe in me, even though they die, will live, and everyone who lives and believes in me will never die. Do you believe this?'* (11:25-26) Jesus' statement calls forth her belief in himself as the Messiah and as the Son of God.

Mary, the other sister, joins them. Mary kneels at the feet of Jesus and also criticises him for his delayed arrival. Seeing her weeping, he asks where the the tomb is. Noting that Jesus is *greatly disturbed*, Alan Culpepper asks, 'Is he angry at death, angry at the people's lack of faith, grieving with or for his friends, or responding to the immediate prospect of his own death?'[1] As they go to the tomb of Lazarus Jesus begins to weep. At the tomb Jesus is again *greatly disturbed*. Following his order for the removal of the stone lying in front of the tomb, he prays aloud and calls forth the dead man, *'Lazarus, come out!'* As the dead man emerges still bound in grave cloths, Jesus tells the onlookers, *'Unbind him, and let him go.'* As a result many believe in Jesus but some report what has happened to opponents of Jesus.

Interpreting the Story

In his treatment of the characters in John 11, Alan Culpepper has tentatively suggested, 'Martha represents the ideal of discerning faith and service, Mary unlimited love and devotion, Lazarus the hope of resurrection life.'[2]

---

[1] R. Alan Culpepper, *The Gospel and Letters of John*, p. 188.

[2] R. Alan Culpepper, *Anatomy of the Fourth Gospel*, p. 142.

'I am the resurrection and the life.'

Resurrection for the Jew meant an embodied and new life for the dead after they have been asleep awaiting the judgement. For the Christian it came to mean the embodied and new life for the crucified Jesus. And it will mean the resurrection of all at the final coming of Christ.

Life for the Jew meant the gift of the creating and sustaining God to all persons and things. For the Christian it came to mean the new life inaugurated and realised by the coming of Jesus and the gift of the Holy Spirit. In simple terms, it's eternal life, God's kind of life.

Elsewhere Jesus promises that God's kind of life is enjoyed here and now by believers, *'Very truly, I tell you, anyone who hears my word and believes him who sent me has eternal life, and does not come under judgement, but has passed from death to life. Very truly, I tell you, the hour is coming, and is now here, when the dead will hear the voice of the Son of God, and those who hear will live.' (John 5:24-25)*

The same power which gives believers eternal life during their earthly existence will, after the death of the body, give renewed existence in the life beyond. As Jesus says, *'Do not be astonished at this; for the hour is coming when all who are in their graves will hear his voice and will come out—those who have done good, to the resurrection of life, and those who have done evil, to the resurrection of condemnation.' (John 5:28-29)*

It should be noted that the temporary resuscitation of Lazarus can be understood to prefigure the final resurrection of the dead. The actual resurrection of Jesus, on the other hand, is the first instalment of the final resurrection of the dead. In the words of Paul, *Christ, being raised from the dead, will never die again (Romans 6:9)* and *Christ has been raised from the dead, the first fruits of those who have died (1 Corinthians 15:20)*. As followers of Jesus, we can thank God that our death is not the end but the entry into new life.

Experiencing the Story

Some years ago as a sorrowing widower I received a letter which included the following helpful words from my former pastor John Claypool: 'I have no words of explanation - only great sadness and empathy for you and your loved ones. I have found in my "valleys of the shadows" that I was mysteriously and graciously sustained and I am confident that will occur for you as well .... But I have more reason than ever to believe in the Resurrection. When we get to the place where we have to say: "If there is any thing more, it is up to God," I have found there is more.'

This pastor had experienced his own severe loss, the illness and eventual death of his young daughter Laura Lue. Yet, in the face of such a calamity, he preached a series of four messages which were later published in a short book of profound insight, *Tracks of a fellow struggler: How to handle grief.* I was privileged to be present to hear three of these sermons. 'The basis of hope'[3] was first preached eleven days after being told that the eight year old girl was suffering from acute leukaemia. The Bible reading that morning was Romans 8:28-39. The sermon included the words: 'The raising of Christ Jesus from the dead is not only the greatest deed of the Bible; it is our basis of hope in the midst of tragedy.'

Thanks to medication the little girl had remission from the disease for nine months before a relapse. Then she had ten days of suffering before she went into remission again. 'Strength not

---

[3] John Claypool, *Tracks of a fellow struggler: How to handle grief*, pp. 19-39.

to faint'[4] was the title of the sermon preached after this experience. The Bible reading was Isaiah 40:27-31. Towards the end of the sermon Claypool said: 'My religion has been the difference in the last two weeks; it has given me the gift of patience, the gift of endurance, the strength to walk and not faint. And I am here to give thanks for that!'

Unfortunately, eighteen months after the initial diagnosis, Laura Lue died at home around Christmas time. It was a month before John Claypool returned to the pulpit. He then preached a sermon entitled 'Life is gift.'[5] The Bible passage was the story of Abraham and Isaac on Mount Moriah in Genesis 22:1-14. He considered three possible roads out of the darkness of the death of his ten year old daughter. First, he chose not to take 'the road of unquestioning resignation.' As Carlyle Marney wrote to him, 'I fall back on the idea that God has a lot to give an account for.' Second, he decided not to follow 'the road of total intellectual understanding.' He agreed with George Buttrick who said, 'Life is essentially a series of events to be borne and lived through rather than intellectual riddles to be played with and solved.' Third, and most significantly, John Claypool chose 'the road of gratitude.' It wasn't easy but he chose to remember that his daughter was a gift and to thank God for such a gift, even though the gift had been taken away.

In the light of all this, I am moved by the words of Jesus: *'I am the resurrection and the life. Those who believe in me, even though they die, will live, and everyone who lives and believes*

---

[4] Ibid., pp. 41-62.

[5] Ibid., pp. 63-83.

in me will never die.' (John 11:25-26)[6] The description of Jesus as *the resurrection and the life* is so powerful. On the one hand, Jesus focuses on the effect of faith on the believer's death. As *the resurrection*, Jesus is saying that he gives spiritual life to the physically dead. On the other hand, Jesus focuses on the effect of faith on the believer's life. As *the life*, Jesus is saying that he does not allow spiritual death to touch those who believe in him.

Reflection

Think about the sort of losses that people experience from womb to tomb.

Prayer

Lord, we thank you that to believe in you in the ups and downs of life is to experience daily renewal and continual purpose and true meaning. Amen.

---

[6] See Doug Rowston, *Jesus and Life*, pp. 29-33.

26 Doubting Thomas

But Thomas (who was called the Twin), one of the twelve, was not with them when Jesus came. So the other disciples told him, 'We have seen the Lord.' But he said to them, 'Unless I see the mark of the nails in his hands, and put my finger in the mark of the nails and my hand in his side, I will not believe.' A week later his disciples were again in the house, and Thomas was with them. Although the doors were shut, Jesus came and stood among them and said, 'Peace be with you.' Then he said to Thomas, 'Put your finger here and see my hands. Reach out your hand and put it in my side. Do not doubt but believe.' Thomas answered him, 'My Lord and my God!' Jesus said to him, 'Have you believed because you have seen me? Blessed are those who have not seen and yet have come to believe.'
(John 20:24-29; Aland, *Synopsis* ## 357, 366)

Telling the Story

As we read this story three things are apparent. First, Jesus knows how Thomas thinks. Thomas in John 14:5 had asked about Jesus' destination, *'Lord, we do not know where you are going. How can we know the way?'* Practical and honest Thomas wanted a road map rather than a compass. On the evening of the day of resurrection Thomas is absent when Jesus appears to the other disciples. Literal-minded and doubt-filled Thomas is told about it but confesses, *'Unless I see the mark of the nails in his hands, and put my finger in the mark of the nails and my hand in his side, I will not believe.'* Yet Jesus lets Thomas have his doubts for a whole week. Thomas' inability to accept the testimony of the other disciples does not exclude him from their fellowship as the disciples allow him, doubts and all, to join them.

Second, Thomas knows Jesus. Thomas in John 11:16 had told his fellow disciples to accompany Jesus back to Judea with the words, *'Let us also go, that we may die with him.'* Realistic and loyal Thomas looked death in the face and chose death with Jesus rather than life without him. On the evening of the day of resurrection when Thomas says, *'Unless I see ... I will not believe'*, he is acknowledging that Jesus' commitment to people has cost him his life. He knows that when people matter more than things life is tough and demanding and this was exemplified in Jesus. After all in John 10:11 Jesus had said, *'I am the good shepherd. The good shepherd lays down his life for the sheep.'* But Thomas is not ready to believe that the good shepherd has the power to take his own life up again.

Third, Jesus makes himself known to Thomas. He says to all the disciples, *'Peace be with you.'* Then he says to Thomas, *'Put your finger here and see my hands. Reach out your hand and put it in my side. Do not doubt but believe.'* Thomas finds peace despite the seeming defeat of the cross. Indeed, it is not Jesus who is defeated, it's the powers of evil and death. Accordingly, Thomas can now only acknowledge Jesus with the memorable words, *'My Lord and my God!'* Finally, Jesus speaks to the present and the future. *'Have you* (singular) *believed because you* (singular) *have seen me? Blessed are those who have not seen and yet have come to believe.'*

An afterthought to the story is worth noting. While Jesus says 'Peace' to all, he says to Thomas 'Look at the evidence'. It could well be that Thomas didn't need the evidence, what he needed was peace. The crucified and risen Jesus brought peace to Thomas. When peace came, the evidence was there but he didn't need it. All Thomas needed to do was to acknowledge Jesus as his Lord and his God.

*'Put your finger here and see my hands.
Reach out your hand and put it in my side.
Do not doubt but believe.'*

Interpreting the Story

In John 20 there is a progression in the levels of believing.[1] First, the Beloved Disciple believes when he sees the empty

---
[1] Raymond E. Brown, *The Gospel of John,* 2:1046.

tomb. *Then the other disciple, who reached the tomb first, also went in, and he saw and believed. (20:8)* All that the Beloved Disciple sees in the empty tomb are the linen wrappings and a head cloth, yet he believes. With Peter he just returns home.

Second, Mary believes when Jesus calls her name. *Jesus said to her, 'Mary!' She turned and said to him in Hebrew, 'Rabbouni!' (which means Teacher). (20:16)* All that Mary hears is the Teacher's voice; then she believes. Sight turns to insight. She goes and tells the disciples whom she has seen and what Jesus has said.

Third, the disciples believe when they see the Lord. *After he said this, he showed them his hands and his side. Then the disciples rejoiced when they saw the Lord. (20:20)* All that they can do is to receive his blessing and commission. Later they tell the absent Thomas. They believe but still Thomas does not.

Fourth, Thomas believes when Jesus says, 'Peace be with you all. Thomas, look at the evidence and stop doubting.' *Then he said to Thomas, 'Put your finger here and see my hands. Reach out your hand and put it in my side. Do not doubt but believe.' (20:27)* Thomas obeys the command, does not touch Jesus, and comes to believe. *Thomas answered him, 'My Lord and my God!' (20:28)* No higher praise can be given to the one who is the Word. The words of Thomas are in tune with the start of John's Gospel: *From the very beginning, when God was, the Word also was; where God was, the Word was with him; what God was, the Word also was. (John 1:1-2*[2]*)*

---

[2] *Today's English Version* First Edition of 1966. This translation eventually became *The Good News Bible.*

Fifth, there are those who have not seen yet believe. *Jesus said to him (Thomas), 'Have you believed because you have seen me? Blessed are those who have not seen and yet have come to believe.' (20:29)* Unlike the Beloved Disciple, Mary, the disciples without Thomas, and Thomas with the disciples, there are those do not see Jesus. Yet they believe ... and receive God's kind of life.

Therefore it is fitting that chapter 20 concludes with the summary: *Now Jesus did many other signs in the presence of his disciples, which are not written in this book. But these are written so that you may come to believe that Jesus is the Messiah, the Son of God, and that through believing you may have life in his name. (20:30-31)*

Experiencing the Story

Paul Tillich was a theologian who experienced demonic forces in his personal and public life. From the trenches of the First World War as a chaplain to the rise of the Nazis to power in the 1930s as a professor in a German university, he experienced anxiety. From the uncertainties of American life during the Depression and through the World War as a refugee in New York City, he continued to experience anxiety. Eventually he produced collections of densely written lectures and sermons.

In one of his published lecture series he made a profoundly significant statement. 'We find that at the end of ancient civilisation ontic anxiety (the anxiety of fate and death) is predominant, at the end of the Middle Ages moral anxiety (the anxiety of guilt and condemnation), and at the end of the modern period spiritual anxiety (the anxiety of emptiness and meaninglessness).'[3]

In our age of spiritual anxiety, of all the characters we meet in the Bible, Thomas may well be the most realistic and helpful model for people who want to believe in the twenty-first century. When we catch ourselves saying, 'I always expect the worst', or 'If it works, and only then, it's all right', or 'I won't believe anything I can't see', then we know that we have a little of Thomas in us. We can take heart that the story of Doubting Thomas tells us that it is all right to have doubts.

Frederick Buechner writes, 'Whether your faith is that there is a God or not, if you don't have any doubts, you are either kidding yourself or asleep. Doubts are the ants in the pants of faith. They keep it awake and moving.'[4] We may have our doubts for a long time. We all need our doubts and fears to give way to certainties and securities. They do in God's good time and in an atmosphere of freedom and acceptance, rather than coercion and compulsion. Despite our doubts and because of God's loving acceptance in Jesus, we learn to have God's kind of life.

During my time as a Religious Education teacher at Prince Alfred College, I remember a class with year 10 students. I began the class by telling the students about my conversation over the weekend with a famous football coach, David Parkin. Parkin had been a student at the same Teachers' College as my first wife. When she was alive she would recall the presence of

---

[3] Paul Tillich, *The Courage To Be*, p. 63.

[4] Frederick Buechner, *Beyond Words*, p. 85.

this up and coming footballer at the college. After a successful playing career Parkin had embarked on a successful coaching career. In time he coached my favourite football team Carlton to three AFL premierships. On that Monday morning I recounted my conversation with Parkin to my somewhat interested Religious Education class. We had talked about our love of teaching. One of the students broke into my story and asked, 'Does he believe in God?' I had to admit, 'We didn't talk about believing in God.' I added, 'So I don't know if he believes in God … but I do know that God believes in him.'

Reflection

Think about the doubts and fears that people encounter today.

Prayer

Lord, when we have feelings of doubt and times of fear, help us to remember the story of Doubting Thomas and his experience of the peace that Jesus gives. Amen.

27 A Stranger on the Shore

After these things Jesus showed himself again to the disciples by the Sea of Tiberias; and he showed himself in this way. Gathered there together were Simon Peter, Thomas called the Twin, Nathanael of Cana in Galilee, the sons of Zebedee, and two others of his disciples. Simon Peter said to them, 'I am going fishing.' They said to him, 'We will go with you.' They went out and got into the boat, but that night they caught nothing. Just after daybreak, Jesus stood on the beach; but the disciples did not know that it was Jesus. Jesus said to them, 'Children, you have no fish, have you?' They answered him, 'No.' He said to them, 'Cast the net to the right side of the boat, and you will find some.' So they cast it, and now they were not able to haul it in because there were so many fish. That disciple whom Jesus loved said to Peter, 'It is the Lord!' When Simon Peter heard that it was the Lord, he put on some clothes, for he was naked, and jumped into the sea. But the other disciples came in the boat, dragging the net full of fish, for they were not far from the land, only about a hundred yards/metres off. When they had gone ashore, they saw a charcoal fire there, with fish on it, and bread. Jesus said to them, 'Bring some of the fish that you have just caught.' So Simon Peter went aboard and hauled the net ashore, full of large fish, a hundred and fifty-three of them; and though there were so many, the net was not torn. Jesus said to them, 'Come and have breakfast.' Now none of the disciples dared to ask him, 'Who are you?' because they knew it was the Lord. Jesus came and took the bread and gave it to them, and did the same with the fish. This was now the third time that Jesus appeared to the disciples after he was raised from the dead.
(John 21:1-14; Aland, *Synopsis* # 367)

Telling the Story

It is after the death and resurrection of Jesus in Jerusalem that seven disciples go back to Lake Galilee. Whereas in John 20 they were among people who came to believe in the risen Lord, it appears in John 21 that they have not put their belief into missionary action. They are informed but not transformed. Simon Peter leads them in going fishing on the lake. After an unsuccessful night's fishing they are greeted by a stranger on the shore. He asks, *'Children, you have no fish, have you?'*

When they admit it, the stranger suggests, *'Cast the net to the right side of the boat, and you will find some.'* How things change! The net is full of fish and the stranger is recognised. The Beloved Disciple tells Peter, *'It is the Lord!'* Impulsive and impetuous Peter puts on some clothes and jumps into the water. The other disciples follow in the boat dragging the full net. Then Jesus says, *'Bring some of the fish that you have just caught.'* All of them, including Peter, haul in the net. They have caught 153 fish! As they gather around a charcoal fire, Jesus says, *'Come and have breakfast.'* None dares to ask him his identity, but they know. Jesus feeds them bread and fish.

Interpreting the Story

At the end of our journey through John's signs, we come to the intriguing story of a miraculous catch of fish by the seven disciples.

Stephen Smalley in his understanding of the structure of the Fourth Gospel sees this event as the seventh sign.[1] He sees associations between Signs, Discourses, and 'I am' Sayings as follows:

---

[1] Stephen Smalley, *John - Evangelist and Interpreter*, p.135.

Sign	Discourse	'I am' Saying
Water into wine (ch. 2)	New life (ch. 3)	The true vine (15:1)
The official's son (ch. 4)	Water of life (ch. 4)	The way, the truth, and the life (14:6)
The sick man (ch. 5)	Life-giving Son (ch. 5)	The door of the sheep (10:7)
The 5000 fed (ch. 6)	Bread of life (ch. 6) and Spirit of life (ch. 7)	The bread of life (6:35)
The blind man (ch. 9)	Light of life (ch. 8)	The light of the world (8:12)
Lazarus (ch. 11)	Life-giving shepherd (ch. 10)	The resurrection and the life (11:25)
The catch of fish (ch. 21)	Disciple life (chs. 14-16)	The good shepherd (10:11)

On the other hand, N.T. Wright lists the signs in John's Gospel differently He understands the crucifixion as the climax of seven days of the old creation. The resurrection comes as an eighth sign and the new creation begins.[2]

---

[2] N.T. Wright, *The Resurrection of the Son of God*, p. 669.

1. Water into wine (2:1-11)

2. The official's son (4:46-54)

3. The paralyzed man at the pool (5:2-9)

4. Multiplication of loaves (6:1-14)

5. The man born blind (9:1-7)

6. The raising of Lazarus (11:1-44)

7. The crucifixion (19:1-37)

8. The resurrection (20:1-29)

The reader will be aware that I have offered a slightly refined version of the signs in the Fourth Gospel. However, the same perspective is being taken as Smalley and Wright. John's Gospel is presenting a number of occasions in which the glory or splendour of God is revealed in Jesus with the result that people truly believe and receive God's kind of life.

As the Fourth Gospel offers the story of a stranger on the shore three themes emerge.[3] First, the net is *full of large fish, a hundred and fifty-three of them.* Is the number an indication of an eyewitness? Or is the number a symbol of fullness? For example, C.K. Barrett observes, '153 is a triangular number, and = 1+2+3 ... +17. 17 itself is the sum of 7 and 10, both numbers which even separately are indicative of completeness and perfection.'[4] Whichever explanation we accept, the number

---

[3] William E. Hull, 'John', *The Broadman Bible Commentary*, 9:373.

[4] C.K. Barrett, *The Gospel According To St. John*, p. 581.

represents abundance for fishermen who had responded to the call of Jesus: *'Follow me and I will make you fish for people.' (Mark 1:17)*

Second, *the net* is *not torn*. Despite the large catch the net stays in one piece. Elsewhere in John's Gospel there are references to unity: the good shepherd's promise of *one flock, one shepherd* (10:16), Jesus' prayer for his future disciples *that they may all be one* (17:20), and included in the crucified's clothes *the tunic was seamless* (19:23). The symbolism is well captured in the comment by Barrett: 'The church remains one, in spite of the number and variety of its members.'[5]

Third, Jesus says, *'Come and have breakfast.'* Jesus invites the seven disciples to join him around the charcoal fire and eat bread and fish that he has miraculously prepared. *Jesus came and took the bread and gave it to them, and did the same with the fish.* One is reminded of the feeding of the five thousand. *Then Jesus took the loaves, and when he had given thanks, he distributed them to those who were seated; so also the fish, as much as they wanted. (John 6:11)* Both that meal for a large crowd and this breakfast for a small group have associations with an invitation to join Jesus in sharing his gifts in word and deed with others. Alan Culpepper says, 'The great catch of fish, therefore, is an epiphany that pictures the missionary task of the church.'[6]

---

[5] Ibid., p. 582.

[6] R. Alan Culpepper, *The Gospel and Letters of John*, p. 247.

Experiencing the Story

Imagine that you are the writer of the Fourth Gospel. You are now putting the final touches to your version of the Good News about Jesus. You decide to give credit where credit is due. You acknowledge your prime source. So you write these words: *This is the disciple who is testifying to these things and has written them, and we know that his testimony is true. But there are also many other things that Jesus did; if every one of them were written down, I suppose that the world itself could not contain the books that would be written. (John 21:24-25)*

Among the things that you, as author and editor, have learned are the signs of Jesus. You are aware of the stories of a wedding, of a royal official, of a lame man, of a large crowd, of the lake, of a blind man, of dead Lazarus, of doubting Thomas, and of a stranger on the shore. And these are only a selection of what could have been told. But the stories are all about the same person, that stranger on the shore. He's the one who is the true vine, the gate, the way and the truth and the life, the bread of life, the good shepherd, the light of the world, the resurrection and the life!

At secondary school, I had a History teacher named Henry Hall. When Doc Hall died the Melbourne Age newspaper printed an obituary which included two quotations. One was from Seneca in the first century: 'It is when the gods hate a man with particular abhorrence that they drive him into the profession of schoolmaster.' The other was from Ian Hay in the twentieth century to the effect that teachers are 'members of the most responsible, the least advertised, the worst paid and the most richly rewarded profession in the world.'

As I grow older I think of Doc Hall with appreciation. His teaching style featured a thoughtful approach to the questions of students. He invariably would answer, 'Well, yes and no.' We could look at historical issues from two sides. Much the same could be said of the first followers of Jesus. They could always think of life before and after meeting Jesus. Before Jesus came into their lives they were in the dark. After they encountered Jesus they knew the truth of the statement: *The light shines in the darkness, and the darkness did not overcome it. (John 1:5)*

At Brighton Grammar I also had an Anglican Headmaster. One day I was asked to report to the Head's study. He had learnt that I had been studying Greek because I was interested in becoming a Baptist minister. So it was on June 19th 1958 that Canon Wilson gave me a Greek New Testament from his private library. In doing so he proved to be a worthy member of the most richly rewarded profession in the world. He also proved to be a true follower of Jesus in helping a young Baptist student follow Jesus into an unknown and uncertain future. The one known and certain thing in the future has turned out to be that the stranger on the shore in John 21 is a stranger no more.

Reflection

Think about the signs of God's glory in the life of Jesus.

Prayer

Lord, you were the stranger on the shore. Help us to know you as a stranger no more but as our way and our truth and our life. Amen.

Conclusion

At the end of our selection of stories about Jesus in the Four Gospels, we are left with a powerful impression of the figure of Jesus. Here is someone who the Gospel writers believed performed signs of God's power, who revealed the splendour of God, who fulfilled the promises of the Old Testament, who spoke words of transformation, and who called ordinary people such as ourselves to follow him on an extraordinary venture. Therefore, in telling and interpreting these stories, we are given opportunities to experience the coming of God's reign and the gift of God's kind of life here and now.

In the Synoptic Gospels as Jesus encounters demonic forces, he is reported to have said, *'If it is by the Spirit of God or the finger of God that I cast out demons, then the Spirit of God has come to you.' (Matthew 12:28; Luke 11:20)* In the Gospels the powers of evil and death are overcome by the words and deeds of Jesus. Furthermore, the Fourth Gospel culminates in a statement about the signs of Jesus. *Now Jesus did many other signs in the presence of his disciples, which are not written in this book. But these are written so that you may come to believe that Jesus is the Messiah, the Son of God, and that through believing you may have life in his name.of the signs that readers may believe and have life. (John 20:31)* Enough has been said to indicate that without the Synoptic miracles and the signs of the Fourth Gospel, the stories about Jesus would be incomplete. Whatever we make of them, they are there to be told, interpreted, and above all, to be experienced.

I trust that readers of this book will not be left with the impression that there is nothing new in my treatment. By way of comparison, I remember the incident in the life of a philosopher, Karl Jaspers, who had not seen the famous New Testament scholar Rudolf Bultmann for many years. After listening to a lecture by Bultmann, Jaspers exclaimed, 'He's still doing the same old thing. There are no surprises and no developments with him. He has learned nothing new. No criticism has ever caused him to revise his position in any way. He sits securely like a windowless monad in the shell of his terminology.'[1]

I also trust that my readers will find my presentation easy to comprehend. Once again a contrast springs to mind. Helmut Thielicke relates the experience of the students of another New Testament scholar, this time Ernst Fuchs. As Thielicke says, 'In complete contrast to his teacher Bultmann, whole sections of Fuchs' speeches would be given over to sibylline cascades of words that nobody understood. That did not make his followers lose faith in him ... The rest of us also realised that some meaning did indeed lie hidden behind these esoteric and dark sayings, for a pearl of thought could suddenly light up in the midst of the amorphous flow of words.'[2]

In conclusion, I encourage seekers after truth to keep reading the stories about Jesus. What was it like to encounter Jesus? Imagine yourself to be a leper cleansed. Visualise being a mentally ill man transformed. Put yourself in the position of a fisherman needing and then finding a catch of fish. Think about being at a wedding where water turns to wine. By putting

---

[1] Helmut Thielicke, *Notes from a Wayfarer*, p. 160.

[2] Ibid., p. 202.

ourselves back into such situations, these stories about Jesus come alive, and so do we. As Paul the Apostle wrote, *So if anyone is in Christ, there is a new creation. (2 Corinthians 5:17)* Yes, God's kingdom and his kind of life open up to us as we face the challenge of the things that Jesus said and did.

Select Bibliography

Aland, Kurt. *Synopsis of the Four Gospels* (United Bible Societies, 1972)
[The essential Greek-English Synopsis]

Bauer, Walter. *A Greek-English Lexicon of the New Testament and Other Early Christian Literature* First edition, 1957, W. F. Arndt & F. W. Gingrich. Second edition, 1979, F. W. Gingrich & F. W. Danker. Third edition, 2000, Frederick William Danker. (University of Chicago Press)
[An indispensable resource]

Matthew

Allison, Jr., Dale C. *Matthew A Shorter Commentary* (T&T Clark, 2004)
[A very helpful shorter version of a three volume academic commentary]

Barclay, William. *The Daily Study Bible: Matthew Vols. 1 & 2* (The Saint Andrew Press, 1975)
[A devotional gem]

Bornkamm, Günther. 'The Stilling of the Storm in Matthew', *Tradition and Interpretation in Matthew* (SCM Press, 1963) pp. 52-57
[A classic essay by a German New Testament scholar]

Long, Thomas G. *Matthew* (Westminster John Knox Press, 1997)
[A very effective study for individuals and groups]

Stagg, Frank. 'Matthew', *The Broadman Bible Commentary* (Broadman Press, 1969) 8:61-253
[An ideal resource for teaching and preaching by an expert in the study of the Greek New Testament]

Witherington, Ben III. *Matthew* (Smyth & Helwys, 2006)
[A very clear and highly accessible commentary]

Wright, Tom. *Matthew for Everyone Parts 1 & 2* (SPCK, 2002)
[A marvellous resource for non-specialist readers]

Mark

Barclay, William. *The Daily Study Bible: Mark* (The Saint Andrew Press, 1975)
[A devotional gem]

Culpepper, R. Alan. *Mark* (Smyth & Helwys, 2007)
[An excellent treatment of the making and meaning of Mark]

Perkins, Pheme. 'The Gospel of Mark', *The New Interpreter's Bible* (Abingdon, 1995) 8:507-733
[A fine piece of work: introduction, commentary, and reflections]

Taylor, Vincent. *The Gospel According To St. Mark* (Macmillan, 1952)
[The best commentary on the Greek text]

Witherington, Ben III. *The Gospel of Mark* (Eerdmans, 2001)
[A helpful socio-rhetorical commentary]

Wright, Tom. *Mark for Everyone* (SPCK, 2001)
[A marvellous resource for non-specialist readers]

Luke

Barclay, William. *The Daily Study Bible: Luke* (The Saint Andrew Press, 1975)
[A devotional gem]

Caird, G.B. *Saint Luke* (Penguin Books, 1963)
[A timeless masterpiece]

Culpepper R. Alan. 'The Gospel of Luke', *The New Interpreter's Bible* (Abingdon, 1995) 9:1-490
[A fine piece of work: introduction, commentary, and reflections]

Green, Joel B. *The Gospel of Luke* (Eerdmans, 1997)
[An insightful commentary on the Greek text]

Marshall, I. Howard. *The Gospel of Luke* (The Paternoster Press, 1978)
[The best commentary on the Greek text]

Wright, Tom. *Luke for Everyone* (SPCK, 2001)
[A marvellous resource for non-specialist readers]

John

Barclay, William. *The Daily Study Bible: John Vols.1 & 2* (The Saint Andrew Press, 1975)
[A devotional gem]

Barrett, C.K. *The Gospel According To St. John* (West-minster Press, 1978)
[A detailed and trustworthy commentary on the Greek text]

Brown, Raymond E. *The Gospel of John Vols.1 & 2* (Doubleday, 1966 & 1970)
[Two encyclopedic volumes on the Fourth Gospel]

Culpepper, R. Alan. *Anatomy of the Fourth Gospel* (Fortress Press, 1983)
[A groundbreaking literary study of John]

_____ *The Gospel and Letters of John* (Abingdon Press, 1998)
[A brilliant introduction and commentary on the Gospel and the Letters]

Dodd, C.H. *The Interpretation of the Fourth Gospel* and *Historical Tradition in the Fourth Gospel* (Cambridge University Press, 1954 and 1963)
[Two major works treating leading ideas, structure, narrative, and sayings of Jesus in the Fourth Gospel]

Hull, William E. 'John', *The Broadman Bible Commentary* (Broadman Press, 1970) 9:189-376
[A brief but brilliantly written commentary by a trustworthy interpreter]

Rowston, Doug. *Jesus and Life: Word Pictures in John's Gospel* (GRACE & PEACE BOOKS, 2021)
[An introduction to key sayings of Jesus in John's Gospel]

Witherington, Ben III. *John's Wisdom* (Westminster John Knox Press, 1995)
[A fine treatment of the original setting and the contemporary meaning]

Wright, Tom. *John for Everyone Parts 1 & 2* (SPCK, 2002)
[A marvellous resource for non-specialist readers]

Biblical Studies

Jeremias, Joachim. *The Rediscovery of Bethesda John 5:2* (Southern Baptist Theological Seminary, 1966)
[A valuable archaeological study]

_____ *Jerusalem in the Time of Jesus* (SCM Press,1969)
[A fine description of first century Palestinian life]

Neill, Stephen. *Jesus Through Many Eyes: Introduction to the Theology of the New Testament* (Fortress Press, 1976)
[A fine treatment of the responses to Jesus in the New Testament]

Rowston, Doug. *A Bird's Eye View of the Bible Second Edition* (GRACE & PEACE BOOKS, 2022)
[A reading guide to the overall Bible story]

_____ *Things that Jesus said: Parables of the Kingdom & Eternal Life* (GRACE & PEACE BOOKS, 2022)
[An introduction to some parables in all four Gospels]

Smalley, Stephen. *John - Evangelist and Interpreter* (Paternoster Press, 1998)
[A study of historical, theological, and literary issues]

Stagg, Evelyn and Frank. *Woman in the World of Jesus* (Westminster Press, 1975)
[Perspectives on the role of women in the time of Jesus]

Walker, Peter. *In the Steps of Jesus* (Lion Hudson, 2009)
[A travel guide to the land of Jesus]

Wright, N.T. *The Resurrection of the Son of God* (SPCK, 2003)
[A comprehensive examination of resurrection in the world of the Bible]

Miscellaneous Materials

Balmer, Randall. *Redeemer The Life of Jimmy Carter* (Basic Books, 2014)
[An analysis of the life and work of Jimmy Carter]

Buechner, Frederick. *Beyond Words* (HarperSanFrancisco, 2004)
[A treasury of words, ideas, and names]

_____ *The Magnificent Defeat* (HarperSanFrancisco, 1985)
[A collection of powerful meditations on biblical passages]

_____ *Now and Then* (HarperSanFrancisco, 1983)
[A second autobiography of a truly great American writer]

Carter, Jimmy. *A Full Life Reflections at Ninety* (Simon & Schuster, 2015)
[The autobiography of the 39th President of the United States]

Claypool, John. *Tracks of a fellow struggler: How to handle grief* (Word Books, 1983)
[A testimony of faith in the face of profound grief]

Cryer, Max. *Love Me Tender: The stories behind the world's favourite songs* (Exisle, 2008)
[The tales of 40 popular songs]

Tony Cupit, Ros Gooden and Ken Manley. *From Five Barley Loaves: Australian Baptists in Global Mission 1864-2010* (Morning Star, 2016)
[The history of Australian Baptist missionary enterprise]

Folley, Malcolm. *A Time To Jump* (HarperCollins, 2001)
[The biography of the triple jump World and Olympic champion]

Gonzalez, Justo L. *The Story of Christianity Vols.1 & 2* (Harper & Row, 1984)
[A crisp retelling of Christian history]

Hillenbrand, Laura. *Unbroken* (Fourth Estate, 2014)
[The biography of the Olympian and prisoner of war, Louie Zamperini]

Hinson, E. Glenn. *A Miracle of Grace* (Mercer University Press, 2012)
[Autobiography of a biblical scholar, church historian, and spiritual guide]

Hollyday, Joyce. *Clarence Jordan Essential Writings* (Orbis Books, 2003)
[The life and thought of a modern prophet]

Lewis, C.S. *Miracles* (Geoffrey Bles, 1947)
[A discussion of the possibility or probability of the miraculous]

Mattingley, Christobel. *Battle Order 204: A bomber pilot's story* (Allen & Unwin, 2007)
[The experience of a young Australian in World War II]

Moltmann, Jürgen. *A Broad Place* (Fortress Press, 2008)
[The autobiography of a truly great theologian in modern times]

Oates, Wayne E. *The Bible in Pastoral Care* (Westminster Press, 1952)
[A guide to the pastoral use of the Bible]

_____ *The Struggle To Be Free* (Westminster Press, 1983)
[Autobiography of the outstanding seminary and university professor]

Rawlins, Clive L. *William Barclay The Authorized Biography* (Eerdmans, 1984)
[The biography of the esteemed Scot]

Thielicke, Helmut. *Notes from a Wayfarer* (Paragon House, 1995)
[The autobiography of a famous German theologian]

Tillich, Paul. *The Courage To Be* (Yale University Press, 1952)
[Lectures on 'Courage' by an existentialist theologian]

Williams, Roy with Elizabeth Meyers. *Mr Eternity The Story of Arthur Stace* (Acorn Press, 2017)
[The story behind the writing of 'Eternity' on the streets of Sydney]

www.ingramcontent.com/pod-product-compliance
Lightning Source LLC
Chambersburg PA
CBHW030256010526

44107CB00053B/1734